Yorkshire Terriers

WENDY BEDWELL-WILSON

Yorkshire Terrier
An Interpet Book

Project Team
Editor: Heather Russell-Revesz
Copy Editor: Ann Fusz
Interior Design: Leah Lococo Ltd. and Stephanie Krautheim
Design Layout: Angela Stanford

First Published in the UK 2007 by
Interpet Publishing
Vincent Lane
Dorking
Surrey
RH4 3YX

ISBN 978 1 84286 162 2

Printed and bound in China.

This book has been published with the intent to provide accurate and authoritative information in regard to the subject matter within. While every precaution has been taken in preparation of this book, the author and publisher expressly disclaim responsibility for any errors, omissions, or adverse effects arising from the use or application of the information contained herein. The techniques and suggestions are used at the reader's discretion and are not to be considered a substitute for veterinary care. If you suspect a medical problem consult your vet.

www.interpet.co.uk

Table of **Contents**

Chapter 1

Why I Adore My

Yorkshire Terrier

Yorkshire Terriers (or "Yorkies" to dog lovers) are top among the most popular pedigree dogs, with their numbers increasing every year. Their popularity is easy to understand: Yorkies are spunky, proud, intelligent, majestic little dogs with long locks of flowing human-like hair, a commanding presence, and an attitude ten times their size. They seem to float under their robe of a coat, gliding alongside their humans from room to room—unless a dragonfly or chew toy happens to distract them.

W**hether you're thinking about adding a Yorkie to your family** or you have already, you're among a burgeoning group of Yorkie lovers worldwide. Keepers of these dogs adore their breed. Yorkies accompany city dwellers in dog-friendly about-town totes. They're loyal companions for elderly folks with limited mobility. They even help in the garden, hearkening back to their ancestor's working-class role as rodent catchers on the farm. Indeed, Yorkshire Terries have charmed their way into our lives.

The ancestors of these dogs laden with silken coats came from a group of terriers owned by weavers in Scotland.

Weaving Through History

It seems appropriate that the ancestors of these dogs laden with silken coats came from a group of terriers owned by weavers in Scotland. During the Industrial Revolution in the late eighteenth century, Scottish weavers moved south to Yorkshire, England, to work in the textile mills. They brought with them their beloved Scotch Terriers from home, a group that included the Paisley Terrier, a 16-pound (7.3 kg) terrier with a blue and tan silky-textured coat, and the Clydesdale Terrier, a 12-pound (5.4 kg) terrier with a long and straight steel blue coat.

These Scotch Terriers were bred with other smaller English terriers—hunters of rats and mice—like the 10-pound (4.5 kg) Waterside Terrier with a silky coat and the 5-pound (2.3 kg)

Manchester Terrier. The Skye Terrier is another possible contributor to the Yorkie lineage, but because records were not kept, it is difficult to know for certain.

These Scottish and English terriers crossed and interbred, culminating in the predecessors to the Yorkie we know today. Huddersfield Ben, the sire of the breed, was born in England in 1865. The best example of the breed at the time, Huddersfield Ben frequently competed in and won dog shows. Though he died in 1871, his progeny began a steadily growing interest in the modern Yorkshire Terrier.

In the mid-1880s, this breed was known as the "Broken-Haired Scottish Terrier." They weighed between 12 and 14 pounds (5.4 and 6.4 kg) and hunted rats and mice. In the late 1880s, England's Kennel Club (KC) renamed these terriers Yorkshire Terriers. From that point forward, the breed's popularity steadily increased, thanks in part to wealthier women in the Victorian era who took to these little silken dogs and used them as companions and ratters.

Also during the late nineteenth century, the United States saw its own Yorkshire popularity boom. Records show that in 1872, Butch was the first Yorkie born in the United States. The Yorkie was recognised as a breed by the American Kennel Club in 1885. A dog named Bradford Harry was the first American Kennel Club (AKC) Champion in 1889—he just happened to be the great-great grandson of Huddersfield Ben.

By 1970, the Yorkshire Terrier was the most popular breed in England. In 1978, a Yorkie took top honours at the prestigious Westminster Dog Show, the only time the breed won Best in Show in the US. In 1997, a Yorkie won Best in Show at Crufts.

That Unmistakable Look

When you think of a Yorkie, what picture pops into your mind? Most people know the Yorkie for his long flowing blue and gold coat, his topknot tied with a perfect bow, and his king-of-the-world airs.

That image resembles the Yorkie's breed standard, or the ideal look that was planned and developed by breeders in the nineteenth century. Representatives from breed clubs

FAMILY-FRIENDLY TIP

The Right Family

Little 10-year-old Sara has been asking for a new pet dog for months. She has had her heart set on a Yorkie, and when the day comes to bring him home, she's overjoyed. Will this relationship work? With the right family and with adult supervision, a Yorkie can thrive in a home with children, especially a child Sara's age. Well-behaved, responsible kids who are old enough to understand that the dog is fragile and prone to nipping when threatened can enjoy life with a Yorkie.

Adult Yorkies rather than puppies are your best bet if your family includes children. Youngsters can be unintentionally rough on pets, which is why many breeders will not place Yorkies in homes with small children. These little dogs may look like tiny stuffed animals, but remember: They are not toys. They are fragile living creatures that can be hurt easily. They are also terriers, and they pack a punch when they feel threatened!

SENIOR DOG TIP

A Long Life Ahead

Yorkies live long lives compared to bigger dogs. A healthy Yorkie will romp and play for up to 15 years—that's a long time to develop a strong relationship with your pet. You'll experience many happy and memorable times during those years. Dogs start the ageing process earlier than humans; some consider 7-year-old dogs to be veterans. When your dog begins showing signs of age, he may slow down a bit. His joints begin losing their elasticity. He might begin suffering from a range of age-related health issues, including arthritis, obesity, diabetes, cancer, deafness, cataracts, or heart disease.

You can make your Yorkie's senior years happy ones by taking him to the vet regularly for geriatric screenings. Feed your dog a healthy diet, give him lots of physical and mental exercise, and groom him regularly. A comfortable bed will ease his achy joints, and lots of attention will make him feel like he is still king of the castle.

compose the written standard to ensure the breed looks the same through time—it is a prescribed description of a perfect Yorkshire Terrier. It makes the Yorkie different from a Chihuahua or a Great Dane, and it has kept the Yorkie breed looking the same for more than a century. Judges also use these standards during dog shows, also known as conformation shows, which recognise the best example of the breed.

Even if you don't want to show your pet in competition, it's fun to look at the Yorkie's standards and be able to interpret them when looking at your pet.

General Appearance

The first thing you see when you glance at a Yorkie is a long shimmering blue and tan coat that flows evenly down the sides of his body from a centre parting. He should have a compact little body that appears symmetrical and balanced, and an attitude that exudes confidence, stamina, and importance.

When you look at your own dog, you'll see these characteristics, too. His coat may not be perfectly groomed, and his attitude might not be overly self-assured, but you'll see the flowing blue and tan locks (if he's an adult), the take-charge way-of-thinking, and the proportionate body that glides into a room and declares it his own.

Head

When you look at the Yorkie's head, it appears relatively small, distinguishing it from medium- and standard-size

Your Yorkie may not stalk vermin, but he will keep his eyes and ears on you, guarding his kingdom and protecting it from two-legged or four-legged strangers.

Body

Weighing in at a mere 7 pounds (3.2 kg) or less, the Yorkie's small but mighty body appears square. This means his legs and the back line of his body, from his shoulders to the hips, should create a square with the ground.

The Yorkie's taut, compact torso holds a strong heart and lungs required for hunting hours at a time. It allows for maneuverability when chasing prey. He also holds his head high so everyone knows who is in charge.

The Yorkie's head appears relatively small, distinguishing him from medium- and standard-size terriers.

terriers, such as West Highland White Terriers or Parson Russell Terriers. With a flat top, the skull is neither domed nor apple-shaped. His muzzle is not long, but it is not so short that it appears snub-nosed. His strong teeth bite evenly and soundly, with either a scissor bite or a level bite. Two sparkling black eyes ringed in black gaze adoringly while two erect ears stand above layers of his spun gold coat.

Before the Yorkie became the ruler of the household, those sharp eyes and attentive ears proved invaluable assets when the little hunter preyed upon rodents and vermin. In addition, his bite had to be solid and strong to grasp and kill a mouse.

Legs and Feet

A Yorkie's legs and feet should be strong and sound in order to carry his body during hours of hunting and chasing. He should have straight forelegs and slightly bent hind legs—straight hind legs could cause excess wear on his knees. Round feet sport black toenails. Breeders generally remove the Yorkie's dewclaws, which are extra toes and claws on the inside of the leg above the paw.

Tail

Yorkies are born with a long tail. When the dog plays, hunts for rodents, or chases insects, he carries his tail

The Yorkie holds his head high so everyone knows who is in charge.

slightly higher than the level of his back. In the US, the tail is customarily docked, which means a portion of it is removed. In the UK, both docked or undocked is acceptable in the show ring. In some places tail docking has been banned, in which case the tail resembles a flag when the dog prances.

Coat

Floor-length sheets of straight, silky, thick hair distinguish the Yorkie from all other breeds. The quality of the hair allows its rich colours to shine, so the standard calls for fine but silky texture that falls perfectly straight. The Yorkie is a single-coated breed, which means he has no undercoat. His hair is moderately long, falling evenly to the floor from the dog's neck to his tail. It can be trimmed short, but those who show Yorkies generally keep the coat long and luxurious.

The hair on the Yorkie's head is long and commonly tied in one or two topknots with bows. The hair from his muzzle is very long, too, but the hair from the tips of his ears and feet are usually trimmed short.

This coat, which legends say resulted from the skills of Scottish weavers—the Yorkie's originators—is like finely spun silk: strong and glossy, reflecting and refracting light, making his coat colour appear even more vibrant and metallic.

Colours

As a puppy, the Yorkie has a black coat with tan around his muzzle, underside, tail and his feet up his legs. The blacks and tans intermingle, segregating and lightening as the dog matures. The black on his saddle turns a dark steely-blue—ideally with no signs of tan or black stragglers. The tan on his head and feet transform into a rich golden colour, darker at the roots and lightening at the tips.

Remember, these descriptions represent the ideal specifications for a Yorkshire Terrier. Every Yorkie is unique, and though your dog may or may not meet these standards, understanding them and why they have

Puppies

Puppies are adorable, but a lot of work and a great responsibility! If you work full-time and no one at home can watch your Yorkie pup, you'll need to hire a dog sitter, who will feed him, play with him and exercise him.

been preserved for the last century will lead to a greater appreciation of your Yorkshire Terrier.

King of the Castle

The Yorkshire Terrier embodies a big dog in a small package. This canine exudes confidence and self-importance—he knows his place as king of the castle! Anyone who meets a Yorkie can immediately see his commanding presence, alert attitude, charming personality, and strong will. He also makes a warm lapdog, a smart guard dog, and a constant companion to whomever is willing to acknowledge that he is in charge.

Most registries categorise dogs into certain groups, depending on their purpose or why they were originally

The Yorkie's coat is like finely spun silk: strong and glossy, reflecting and refracting light.

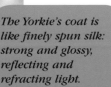

Why I Adore My Yorkshire Terrier

Yorkies will retain their terrier instincts, so you must always supervise them with other small pets.

developed. Yorkies fall into the Toy Group, whose main function is to be a companion or lap dog, according to the KC, and "embody sheer delight," as it states in the AKC group description. While they certainly bring joy and delight to their owners, remember Yorkies are terriers and still retain their terrier instincts. Any new or potential Yorkie owner should be prepared for this tiny terrier with a big presence.

The Toy Terrier

Terriers' personalities precede themselves. Generally speaking, they are energetic, spirited dogs whose ancestors hunted and killed vermin. Most terriers retain this gusto. As a group, they range in size from the smaller West Highland White Terrier (14 to 21 pounds/6.4 to 9.5 kg) to the large Airedale Terrier (43 to 60 pounds/19.5 to 27.2 kg). No matter their size, terriers require dedicated

owners who are ready to deal with a lively personality.

Yorkies, like other terriers, do not fair well with additional pets. Their inflated sense of presence makes them think they can stand up to larger dogs, which may result in an injured or lost pet. And because their ancestors hunted small vermin and rodents, any reptile, small mammal, or cat may not be safe in a house with a Yorkie.

They can also be stubborn and strong-willed. If your Yorkie doesn't want to give that toy back, don't expect him to! Training methods that include positive reinforcement tactics, however, can keep this dog well-mannered.

Despite their spirited and feisty ways, Yorkies make wonderful watchdogs and companions. Protecting their human with their keen sense of hearing and forewarning them of other two-legged or four-legged visitors, these dogs alert their owners with a sharp little bark. Yorkies are also curious creatures, right at home investigating the garden, going for long walks with their owners, or even hunting around the house for their missing chew toy. When their busy day comes to a close, they'll curl up in their owners' lap and await their daily doting.

As owners of Yorkies will attest, these little dynamos delight, entertain, and bring joy to any household—from small apartments and nursing homes to large families with children.

Part of the Yorkie Club

As the popularity of tiny portable dogs has risen to heights surpassed only by the fashionable totes they're carried in, celebrities and sports legends have led the way in touting these toy breeds' beloved traits.

Some popular celebrities who have enjoyed life with a Yorkie include:
- Naomi Watts: Before she met King Kong, Watts befriended a Yorkie named Bob.
- Britney Spears: When she was a child, and before she had her own child, Spears had a Yorkie named Baby.
- Justin Timberlake: Spears' fellow Mousketeer had a Yorkie named Bella.
- Richard Nixon: Pasha the Yorkie lived in the White House for a time.
- Kirsten Dunst: This Spiderman actress shared part of her life with Beauty.

- Mariah Carey: This Grammy winner once owned a Yorkie named Ginger.
- Audrey Hepburn: This famous actress shared her life with Mr. Famous.
- Joan Rivers: Spike and Veronica kept this comedienne laughing.
- Demi Moore: Louie, a Yorkie-Chihuahua cross, was part of Moore's life before Ashton Kutcher.
- Mandy Moore: This musician once had two Yorkies.
- Ivana Trump: She had a Yorkie named Dodo.
- Gisele Bundohen: Vida shared its life with this fashion model.
- Brett Farve: This sports legend tossed footballs with his Yorkie, Jazzmin.
- Jennie Finch: Prada lived her life with Finch, a 2004 Olympic pitcher.

The Expert Knows

The Adoption Option

Have you considered adopting an adult or a rescued Yorkie? Often, these dogs are already housetrained, their bladders have fully developed, and they know how to ask to go to their toilet area. They're also usually trained, or they're willing to learn how to Sit, Stay and Come when called, and their personalities are fully developed. But the best reason of all to consider adopting an adult: You're saving an animal's life. Rescue organisations can pair you with the perfect adult Yorkie.

Chapter **2**

The Stuff of Everyday
Life

Shopping for your pet, which is more and more like shopping for a small furry member of the family, can be a fun but daunting experience! A walk through any pet shop or superstore, a flip through any catalogue, or even browsing online proves that as pets have established themselves in our homes, retailers have responded by offering everything from diamond-studded collars to posh doggie beds to diets formulated specifically for your Yorkie.

To help curb some of your impulse spending on designer totes and tiny sombreros for your Yorkie, here's a list of must-have products for your dog. Different brands and qualities run the gamut, as do costs. Shop around, but don't sacrifice quality for price. Remember: This is your four-legged baby you're shopping for, and he deserves the best!

Home Sweet Home: The Crate

One of the first items you'll need is a crate. Not only does it provide for easy transport to and from the vet's surgery, but it also serves as a house-training tool, a cozy dog den, and place to hide when rambunctious children come to visit.

Crates and kennels come in a wide variety of materials, including plastic, nylon, powder-coated wire, and stainless steel. The hard-sided plastic and fibreglass models, which are generally lighter and more portable, frequently double as airline-approved carriers if required (check with your airline to be certain). They will also keep your Yorkie warmer in the winter. The wire and stainless steel varieties allow for more air flow during hot summers, but they don't provide the privacy your Yorkie might want.

Your dog should be able to stand up, turn around, lay down and stretch out in his kennel. Yorkies enjoy a cozy den-like area rather than vacuous space. Though you may want to give your Yorkie an entire room of his own, he prefers to feel enclosed in his crate.

When you bring the crate home, put it together and make sure the pieces fit properly, the door latches correctly, and the handle works as it should. Also check for any sharp spots that might cut your Yorkie. Lay down a washable fleece lining or blanket to create a comfy space for your pup.

Carry Me!

In addition to a crate, many small dog owners purchase a portable soft-sided carrier. These about-town totes resemble trendy purses or shoulder bags, and they feature a range of accoutrements, such as a mobile phone holder and pockets for keys, your wallet, dog treats, and plastic bags.

Yorkshire Terriers

FAMILY-FRIENDLY TIP

Dog Duty

You and your family will need to divide responsibilities to ensure all your dog's needs are cared for. Choose appropriate family members to take charge of these regular tasks:
- Feeding
- Refilling the water bowl
- Toileting duty
- Exercise/Playtime
- Handling
- Grooming
- Training
- Health

Like crates, each bowl material has its benefits and drawbacks. Plastic bowls are lightweight and inexpensive, but they retain residue and harbour bacteria as they break down. Also, if your Yorkie is a chewer, he could end up ingesting little plastic pieces as he gnaws on the bowl. If you choose plastic, purchase a harder dishwasher-safe plastic and replace it often.

Custom ceramic pieces are beautiful and can match virtually any décor. They are heavier than plastic, so they're not likely to tip over or be turned into a toy. They are more expensive and

Some of these are also airline approved, so you can take your Yorkie with you as you traipse across the country.

Designer carriers in fashionable models and materials often come with a removable fleece liner for easy cleaning and comfort, as well as matching collars, leads, and food bowls, creating a coordinated look for your Yorkie. There's no reason why you and your dog can't be cosmopolitan! Just keep in mind that your Yorkie still needs exercise—you don't want to carry him everywhere.

Feed Me!

Food and water bowls for dogs vary as much as dinnerware patterns for humans. From custom-painted ceramic ware and hand-thrown pottery to sleek stainless steel bowls and durable plastic diners, doggy dining has as much personality as Yorkies themselves.

The Expert Knows

Modern Marvels

Modern conveniences make feeding your dog easier, too. From timed feeders and flowing fountains filled with filtered water, a range of automated products take the guesswork out of meal time. Before you invest in any of these items, however, discuss them with your vet. They may be convenient, but if one should malfunction, it could be hazardous to your Yorkie.

17

The Stuff of Everyday life

breakable, however, and if they're made overseas they may contain lead, which can be harmful to your Yorkie. Make sure any piece you choose is sturdy, lead-free, and dishwasher-safe.

Stainless steel bowls, though the most expensive, clean and sanitise easily. They're heavy enough that your Yorkie won't wander off with it, and they're virtually indestructible. Some designs include rubber bases to keep them from sliding.

Your Yorkie won't be eating that much, so several small bowls are all you'll need. Keep some spares handy so you can wash them regularly. You don't want your pup to be without!

Lead Me!

Soon after he comes home, your Yorkie will need a collar and lead.

Collars

Collars make more than a fashion statement; they also hold your dog's ID tag, which lists your contact information should he ever get lost. Collars also attach to the lead, which you'll need to safely walk your Yorkie.

For your puppy's first few collars, the adjustable nylon types with a buckle will suffice. They come in a variety of colours and styles to fit your Yorkie's

personality. To find the right size, either measure the diameter of your Yorkie's neck and add 2 inches (5 cm) for some growing room, or take your Yorkie to the pet store and try some on. Plan to buy several collars as your Yorkie grows.

After your Yorkie is fully grown, decorative collar choices run the gamut. You can buy a diamond-encrusted leather collar, a colourful vinyl collar, or even a studded motorcycle-dog collar! Some Yorkie owners buy collars to match outfits or to celebrate seasons.

Whatever you choose, be sure the collar is sized and weighted appropriately for your Yorkie—big heavy collars could catch on objects and choke your Yorkie, while small cat collars could be too restrictive. Other collars, such as slip chain collars designed for training purposes, are inappropriate for Yorkies. They're too heavy for their small necks and should only be used with guidance from a professional trainer.

Leads

The lead attaches to the collar, giving you control during walks or obedience training. They often coordinate with the collar and come in matching materials, styles, and sizes. When you purchase a lead, check the attachment to be sure it will not break or unhook from the collar, and choose one with a strong and comfortable loop for your hand.

Like collars, lead choices include an array of lengths, styles, and materials including nylon, hemp, cotton, leather, and vinyl. For your Yorkie's first few leads, a short 4-foot (1.2 m) nylon, cotton webbing, or leather variety is all you'll need. As you begin obedience training, you'll need longer leads, including 6-foot (1.8 m) and 15-foot (4.6 m) varieties.

Harness

Harnesses offer another option for your Yorkie. Because small toy breeds are vulnerable to collapsed tracheas, a harness, which encircles the dog's torso instead of his neck, is an excellent alternative for walking your Yorkie. The lead attaches to the back of the harness instead of the collar, putting the pressure around his body instead of his neck.

Play With Me!

Yorkies love their toys. They wrestle with them, carry them from room to room, and chew them until they're unrecognisable. Yorkies are intelligent, busy dogs, and they need the stimulation that toys provide.

Like every other section in the pet store, the toy choices seem endless. From squeaky balls and figurines shaped like your favourite politician to colourful ropes, stuffed animals, and stuff-able hard rubber balls, there's a toy for any dog's taste.

Despite the choices, Yorkies should only be offered toys that are sized appropriately for their diminutive bodies. Imagine your 7-pound (3.2 kg) Yorkie wielding a Great Dane-sized toy! An increasing number of companies

FAMILY-FRIENDLY TIP

Childhood Chores

Sara had been enjoying her first weeks of life with her new Yorkie puppy, Ruby. She helped her mother with Ruby's housetraining, feeding, and grooming, though the child begged to do more. Sara and Ruby seemed inseparable—until school started. Now, Sara is at school all day, she has homework to do in the evening, and friends to e-mail at night. She doesn't have the same amount of time to dedicate to her four-legged friend.

Sara wanted to take on the responsibility of caring for her puppy, but her mother understood that children should not be the sole caretakers of dogs. Children lose interest in things quickly, and a puppy is not a responsibility to be taken lightly.

Instead, Sara's mother delegated specific puppy-related chores to her. She is teaching her child responsibility, Ruby is reliably cared for, and Sara is enjoying her puppy—and her friends.

Yorkies love to play with balls, but this might be a bit too big for your little dog!

dogs, and toys that require them to work or think will keep them busy for hours. Treat-filled hard rubber toys are up for the task. They will also teach your Yorkie to chew the toy and not your favourite pair of slippers.

Toys are fun, and it will be tempting to give your Yorkie all the toys at once, but don't give in! Keep a secret stash of toys, and dole them out as your dog destroys them.

Contain Me!

X-pens, playpens, and baby gates corral curious puppies. A must for any new puppy owner, containment devices keep your Yorkie in a confined area where he can be monitored and housetrained. If you are unable to keep

manufacture toys designed just for small dogs, like small-sized balls, stuffed animals, and rope toys, so ask for them when you visit your local pet store.

Safety First

When you bring the toys home, check for potential hazards, such as small pieces that could fall off and be ingested. Choose toys that are strong, durable, and well-made. Your Yorkie won't destroy toys like some dogs can, but you still want to ensure your pet's safety.

If your Yorkshire Terrier does demolish his squeaky toy, exposing the noisemaker, replace the toy. Also replace or repair toys whose stuffing is falling out, or whose rope strands are overly frayed. You don't want your Yorkie eating anything he shouldn't!

Keep Him Busy

Yorkies are intelligent

A playpen can confine your pup to a specific area.

your eyes on your Yorkie, pens and gates offer an excellent short-term solution.

X-pens are essentially portable wire panels that confine your pup to a specific area. They can be adjusted to fit any space or size. Often, a dog owner will use these to enclose the pup, his crate, food and water bowl, and toys. Playpens, much like those for human babies, serve a similar purpose. Both the x-pen and the playpen can be taken outside so your Yorkie can enjoy a little sunshine.

Baby gates will give your Yorkie a little more freedom. They confine your pup to one room or one part of the house, keeping the rest off limits. They easily attach to door frames and can be conveniently removed.

Beautify Me!

Taming that Yorkie coat requires daily, weekly, and monthly regimes involving washing, brushing, and clipping. Your Yorkie will also needs his toenails trimmed, ears cleaned, teeth brushed, and top knot perfectly tied. Before your Yorkie comes home, have all of your primping products ready. The sooner you can introduce your dog to the grooming routine, the better. (See Chapter 4, "Looking Good.")

Grooming Tools

You'll need a pin brush and a comb to tame and smooth your Yorkie's lustrous coat. A pin brush is rubber-backed with fine pins which may or may not have small rubber balls on the ends. Choose a metal or stainless steel comb with narrow teeth on one side and wider teeth on the other.

There are many shampoo and conditioner options. Some contain botanicals and aroma-therapeutic ingredients, while others have oatmeal,

A brush is just one of the grooming items you'll need to keep your Yorkie looking good.

fruit essences, and aloe vera. Coat conditioning sprays beautify the coat in between washings and help to tame the tangles.

Toenail clippers, a de-matting comb, small scissors and a blow dryer should be part of your grooming arsenal, too. You'll also need cotton buds and cotton-wool balls to clean your Yorkie's ears and eyes.

As soon as your Yorkie's permanent teeth come in, he will need his teeth

brushed several times a week with a child's toothbrush and dog toothpaste to clean his mouth of bacteria, plaque, and tarter. Toy breeds have weaker gums than standard breeds, and poor dental hygiene has been linked to heart and kidney disease.

Combine all these items in a tote or container for easy access. You'll also want to designate a specific area in your home for grooming so your Yorkie will learn what to expect.

The grooming regime may seem like a lot of work, but with regular maintenance, you'll soon look forward to spending some quality primping time with your pet!

Tag Me!

Your Yorkie will require some identification, and there are several options from which to choose: ID tags, tattoos, and microchips. They each have their benefits and drawbacks, so the best option is to use a combination of at least two.

ID Tags

ID tags are readily visible on your dog's collar. They list your dog's name and your name, address, and telephone number. Styles include plastic, engraved metal, and reflective tags in all shapes, sizes, and colours. They can be ordered from your vet or purchased at your local pet store. These tags are the most common form of identification, and they are often used to reunite a lost dog and owner. If you have several collars for your Yorkie, be sure each one has an ID tag.

ID tags can fall off the collar, and sometimes the engraving wears off, the imprint fades, or it becomes too thin to read. So check the ID tags regularly and make sure that they have your most current information on them.

Tattoos

Tattoos are another identification option. A unique number is tattooed on your Yorkie's skin, typically on his belly or inner thigh. It is then registered with one of several national tattoo databases. When your dog is found, the rescue centre contacts the registries and matches the tattoo number to you.

Microchips

A small rice-sized microchip is another method of identifying your Yorkie. Injected by your veterinary surgeon between your dog's shoulder blades, this microchip contains a certain code that is read by a handheld scanner. The code is stored in a database, and that database registers your name, phone number, and contact information.

Because there are several registries for both the tattoos and the microchips, the registries may provide a tag with a free phone number on it. If you should move or change your phone number, you'll need to notify the appropriate registry.

Tuck Me In!

Everyone loves a comfy bed, and Yorkies are no exception. You'll want to give your pup a warm cozy place of his own to lay his head.

Beds come in all shapes and sizes. Round beds, square beds, basket-style beds filled with cushions, and even beds that look like mattresses are available. The beds are frequently stuffed with cotton, poly-blends, or memory foam, along with cedar chips for odour and insect control. Materials covering the beds are often removable and washable.

As with the other Yorkie essentials, purchase a bed that is sized appropriately for your dog. You want him to feel cozy and safe, and a big giant bed won't give your pup that satisfaction.

While you're housetraining your Yorkie, you may have him sleep in his crate. Bumper beds covered in fleece or sheepskin are designed to fit inside his crate and keep him warm and cozy while he's sleeping the night—or day—away. Be sure they're washable, however, because if he has an accident, you'll want to be able to keep his bedding sanitary.

ID For Your Yorkie

In the UK, all dogs should wear some form of ID. Most local authorities employ a dog warden and it is his/her job to attempt to reunite lost dogs with their owners. However, if the warden picks up a dog without ID, the owner, once located, could face a fine.

The best plan is for your Yorkie to wear a visible form of ID, such as a disc attached to the collar, and back this up with a permanent form of ID, which could be a tattoo or a microchip.

Don't Forget Yourself!

Shopping for your Yorkie can be fun. As the pet product market continues to grow and specialise, you'll find more products out there to make your

SENIOR DOG TIP

New Family, New House

Older dogs who find new homes later in life have a unique set of challenges not experienced by puppies. Because they're older, they may take more time to get used to their new surroundings. They may be disoriented, sedate, and just want to sit back and observe everyone.

Here are some things you can do to make your older dog's homecoming a happy one:
1. Introduce him slowly to the house, showing him the kennel area, the toileting area, and the bedroom.
2. Stay close by to let him know you're around.
3. If he wants to play, be ready!
4. Make sure he has a big, comfy bed. Put it in your bedroom so he can feel secure if he wakes up at night.
5. Be patient and give your veteran dog time to acclimatise.

Yorkie's life better and fuller than ever before. From dog bakeries and day spas to Yorkie-sized clothing and jewellery, you can spoil your pet to your heart's delight.

While you're spoiling your Yorkie, spoil yourself, too, with key chains, t-shirts, paintings, trinkets, and coffee mugs that portray your beloved pet—like any proud parent would!

Puppy Proofing

Now that you know the essential stuff your Yorkie needs, you'll also need to know how to protect him from the stuff already in your home. Preparing your home for a puppy—especially a Yorkie puppy—can be a challenge. Your Yorkie will investigate everything and won't discriminate between valuable antiques and his favourite chew toy!

So let's look at your house from your puppy's point of view—on your hands and knees!

Kitchen

The kitchen has all sorts of interesting cabinets, crawl spaces, nooks, and crannies. If a cabinet can open, your Yorkie will explore everything inside, so install some child-proof latches and try not to store poisonous items in the lower cabinets, just in case. The rubbish bin is another lure, tempting any Yorkie to topple it. Keep the rubbish inside a latched cabinet or secure the can with a locking lid. Yorkies are smart, and they will find a way to jump up on the counter and eat that leftover roast. Be diligent about putting food away. Cords and wires look like fun playthings to a pup, so secure those in Yorkie-proof PVC pipes, staple them down or secure them behind furniture.

Bathroom

The bathroom can be a dangerous place for a Yorkie. If any razors, medications, cotton-wool balls, soaps, or lotions are left within reach, the pup can easily ingest them. Anything he can put in his mouth, he will; so everyone in the family will need to be conscious about cleaning up after themselves. The toilet lid should also be closed at all times because a curious Yorkie could jump in and drown. Install child-proof latches on bathroom cabinets, and secure any cords and wires.

Bedroom

Your Yorkie will gravitate toward anything with your scent. Shoes, slippers, and dirty clothes are fair game, but bits of those things, like a piece of shoestring, could accidentally be swallowed. Keep your clothes picked up, and put your dirty clothes in a tall hamper. Put jewellery, rubber bands, coins, and other items away in drawers or boxes, and secure any cords and wires.

Office

The office is full of papers, magazines, cords, wires, and all sorts of other Yorkie temptations. Your Yorkie might think paper clips, rubber bands, staples, and pens are fun to play with, but they could injure him if swallowed. Anything decorative and mobile will be treated as a toy, so put those things up high or in drawers or file cabinets.

These are just a few suggestions of what your Yorkie might come across. Do a thorough inspection of your home, and if your Yorkie should swallow or injure himself in any way, do not hesitate to call your vet.

When You Can't Be There

Yorkie owners who work often employ dog sitters or dog walkers to entertain their pups while they're away. These professionals care for their pets, and give the dog owners the peace of mind that their four-legged babies are safe and secure.

When you interview potential sitters or walkers, be sure to get the following information:

1. Qualifications and experience
2. References
3. Insurance and/or bonding
4. Emergency pet care experience
5. Security
6. Contract and cost

The Stuff of Everyday life

Chapter 3

Good Eating

Your Yorkie's diet gives him the gusto he needs to get through the day. These diminutive dogs with their tiny stomachs require a healthy diet that will give them the right amount of nutrition in a small package. With so many choices available from your local pet store, how do you choose which diet is best?

Young pups need a diet formulated for growth.

There are the generic and premium brands that vary in price and size. There are the dry food formulas and canned concoctions in hearty rich gravy. There are the trendy organic diets and raw choices that hearken back to the days when dogs hunted prey. There are even the diets that the dog owner makes from scratch! Despite the variety, they should all contain basic nutrients that the canine species requires.

Yorkies, like all other dogs, are carnivores, which means they eat a protein-based diet. Before they became the domesticated pets that we know today, dogs scavenged and preyed on small animals. They also foraged for food, eating berries, grains, and other plant matter when necessary. This diet gave them the protein, fat, carbohydrates, vitamins, and minerals needed for a complete healthy diet.

As a house pet, your Yorkie still requires these basic nutrients. Depending on his age, each dog has different requirements. Young pups need a diet formulated for growth; adults need a diet formulated for maintenance.

Price varies dramatically between brands of dog food. Though all dog food manufacturers must follow basic guidelines, the more expensive, or premium, varieties often exceed those specifications and, therefore, cost more. The ingredients are higher-grade, come from whole-food sources, and contain fewer fillers than the less-expensive labels.

The premium brands frequently contain added nutrients, too, such as antioxidants and vitamin supplements, which benefit veteran dogs, overweight dogs, or toy breeds like your Yorkie. Generally speaking, you will get what you pay for when it comes to dog food—but don't presume expensive is better. Your veterinary surgeon can help you choose a diet that is suitable for your Yorkie.

Nutrient Know-How

Dogs require certain amounts of protein, carbohydrates, fat, vitamins, and minerals to support their normal bodily functions. Let's take a closer look at each type of required food source and how it keeps your Yorkies healthy and happy.

Protein

In many premium brands of dog food, protein is the first ingredient listed. Beef, chicken, turkey, lamb, or duck are the proteins most often used. Other sources include fish, fish meal, liver, eggs, milk, and milk products.

Some grains and beans, such as rice, wheat, corn, barley, and soya also contain protein. They're not complete sources of protein like animal protein, but when combined with other types

FAMILY-FRIENDLY TIP

Kids in the Kitchen

Little 10-year-old Sara looks forward to feeding Ruby every day. She gets out her Yorkie's dry food and food bowl, carefully measures the right amount of food, pours it in the bowl, and lets her puppy eat.

Children can be a great help when it comes to their Yorkie's feeding times. Here are some ways they can get involved:

- Go to the pet store and look at pet food labels with your child. Ask him or her to identify the protein source or the fibre source. Make the food choice together.
- Have your child be in charge of watching the clock. When it's dinner time, ask him or her to sound the alarm.
- Put your child in charge of the food bowl. It will be his or her job to get it out, fill it, clean it, and put it away.
- Let your child measure out the correct amount of food for his or her pet.
- Ask your child to keep an eye on his or her Yorkie's waistline and let you know if it's looking a little fuller than usual.
- Put your child in charge of emptying, cleaning, and refilling your Yorkie's water bowl every day.

Good Eating

Always have clean, fresh water available for your Yorkie.

of food, they can provide many of the amino acids required by dogs.

Yorkie puppies thrive on foods that contain about 28 percent protein; adult Yorkies typically maintain on foods that contain 22 percent protein. Their bodies use it for growing and developing hair and skin, producing hormones, building muscle mass, regulating metabolism, and healing damaged tissue.

Carbohydrates

Carbohydrates, which are sugars and starches found in plant foods, provide the quick energy Yorkies need to exercise and play. They also provide fibre, which is essential for proper bowel function. Common sources of fibre are grains, peas, pasta, and even potatoes.

Carbohydrates, however, are also used as fillers. They are cheaper than protein, so dog food manufacturers use corn and rice to bulk up the foods sold at a less-expensive price. Premium foods often contain high-quality complex carbohydrates to give the dog fibre and sustained energy.

Too many cereal grains could result in a hyped-up Yorkie. If your Yorkie is bouncing off the walls, take a look at how many carbohydrates are in his diet. The fillers will also cause your dog to defecate more often, which means more trips to the toileting area.

Fats

Fats and oils do more than make foods taste good. They provide energy and help your Yorkie feel satisfied. Fats are needed to metabolise fat-soluble vitamins, such as vitamins A, D, K, and E. Unsaturated fatty acids, such as oleic and linoleic acids, also support skin and coat health. They make your Yorkie's coat shimmer and shine.

Yorkie diets may contain anywhere from 8 percent to 18 percent fat, depending on the manufacturer. If your Yorkie's coat is looking dull, consider a food that has more unsaturated fats. If he's looking a little overweight, switch to a low-fat diet after talking with your veterinary surgeon.

Vitamins

In addition to the proteins, carbohydrates, and fats, Yorkies require vitamins, which help the body fight disease, absorb minerals, regulate metabolism, and grow and

function normally. Plant and animal foods naturally contain vitamins. The body maintains and stores fat-soluble vitamins in the body's liver and fatty tissues, and water-soluble vitamins, such as vitamins B and C, are flushed out daily and must be replaced. The right balance of vitamins is crucial to the health and well-being of your Yorkie.

Minerals

Minerals, such as calcium, iron, phosphorous, and nitrate are elements and inorganic compounds the body needs for proper growth and function. Dogs require seven major minerals and 15 trace minerals, including copper and potassium. They help maintain the salt levels in the bloodstream and build bones and

To Supplement or Not?

You take your daily multivitamin to provide you with those extra vitamins and minerals you lack in your diet or use throughout the day. In many pet stores, you'll find an array of dog vitamins, supplements, herbal remedies, and more to give your Yorkie energy, calm him down, or ease his stiff joints. Should you feed them to your pet?

Supplements shouldn't be necessary if you're feeding your dog a well-balanced diet. Commercial diets typically contain all the vitamins and nutrients your Yorkie needs to stay healthy. Puppies and adult dogs generally don't require supplements if they're being fed a commercial diet. Veteran dogs may benefit from some added vitamins to help with kidney function and joint pain. Consult your vet for advice.

If you're feeding a non-commercial diet, however, supplements could be necessary to ensure your pet is getting his minimum requirements of vitamins and minerals. When you develop the diet with a veterinary nutritionist, he or she can help you find the right sources for the supplements, including herbs, eggs, and Brewer's yeast.

The Expert Knows

Water Water Everywhere!

Like humans, dogs' bodies require plenty of water to function normally. Water keeps their digestive systems working, their mucous membranes lubricated, and their cells replicating. It flushes their systems and keeps their bodies free from harmful toxins. Dogs need water to live. With normal play and exercise, your Yorkie will need to replenish his water supply frequently. Always have plenty of fresh, cold water available for your Yorkie.

teeth. Like vitamins, minerals must be balanced for good health.

Commercial Foods

Now that you understand the importance of the ingredients in your Yorkie's food, let's take a look at the different meal options available at the market. Three commercial types are sold at most supermarkets and pet stores: dry food, semi-moist, and canned.

No matter the form, each little morsel of food for Yorkies and other toy breeds should be packed with nutrients. Because they have such tiny mouths and stomachs, they require smaller pieces of food than larger dogs. Those smaller pieces must contain all the nutrients and calories they need to keep them going. Dog food companies know this, so when they develop diets for small dogs, they put as much nutrition as possible in each bite.

Dry Food (Kibble)

It might not look too appetizing to humans, but dry food is delicious to dogs. The food's shape, size, texture, smell, and taste has been researched and tested by scientists and veterinary nutritionists. They develop recipes, conduct feeding trials, and check for complete nutrition to ensure that the food meets their standards.

Yorkies digest dry food easily. Made by cooking the ingredients together in big batches, extruding it into bite-size pieces, and baking it, dry food is often the least expensive food on the shelf. Because it is baked, dry food can be left out in your Yorkie's bowl all day without spoiling. And the crunch of the dry food helps keep your dog's teeth tartar-free.

For Yorkies who have dental problems, are recovering from surgery, or are just finicky, however, dry food poses a challenge. They can't bite into or digest the hard pieces of food, or the dried morsels aren't appealing enough for a picky dog's discriminating taste. These dogs might require a semi-moist or canned food instead.

Semi-moist Food

Semi-moist foods are soft to the bite with a texture resembling Play Dough. They come in all shapes and sizes, from dry food-size morsels and patties to whimsical shapes that look more like treats than food. They often come in resealable bags to keep the moisture locked in.

Like the dry foods, semi-moist foods are formulated to serve the nutritional needs of the dog. The benefit of semi-moist compared to the dry is the water content, which makes it easier for elderly dogs or those with dental problems to chew. The food also smells more appetising to finicky dogs.

To give the semi-moist food that look and texture, however, it often contains a number of chemicals, artificial sweeteners, and colours. Be sure to read the label and check the food's nutritional content before feeding. A high amount of corn syrup or artificial sweetener can be harmful to your Yorkie's metabolism.

Canned Food

Big chunks of meat in hearty rich gravy appeal to not only the dogs, but the humans, too, who may want to give their pets something that resembles "real" food. Available in myriad flavours,

combinations, and recipes, canned foods combine the protein, carbohydrates, fats, and water in a way that caters to many dogs' taste buds. It might not smell or look good to humans, but many dogs like it.

Canned food has a high water content—up to 70 percent water by weight—which supplies the Yorkie with much-needed water. Its taste attracts finicky eaters, it is easier to bite and chew than dry food, and it comes in small quantities for small diets. Canned food has a long shelf life and works well for dogs travelling to shows or obedience competitons.

Despite its benefits, canned food generally costs more. It can not be left out like dry food as it can spoil, and leftovers must be refrigerated. Some Yorkie owners worry about what animal parts are used in the canned food, not to mention the additives and preservatives. Also, it can cause diarrhoea in some dogs.

In addition to the common brands of foods, most pet specialty stores also carry dry and canned or jarred foods in "organic" or "natural" varieties, or those that may be "fit for human consumption." What does this mean?

People food is not always right for dogs— do your research and find out what is healthy for your Yorkie.

What's Right For Your Yorkie?

Different dogs require different diets. Generally, Yorkie breeders recommend dry foods for their dogs. Premium foods made with wholesome ingredients will offer greater nutrition in a smaller package. Yorkies don't eat a lot, so what they do eat should be high quality, nutrient packed, and appealing to them.

Before feeding your Yorkie any food, talk to your breeder and vet, and read the label on any food you are considering for your dog. Be sure your Yorkie is getting the right nutrients from quality sources.

If you have any questions about your Yorkie's diet, call the telephone number on the food's label and talk to the company representative. They'll be happy to answer any question you may have.

The organic trend has moved into the pet market. Popular with human foods, organically grown meats, produce, and grains are grown without the use of pesticides, chemicals, or other such means. Many dog owners believe that feeding their pets a diet free from those additives will benefit and extend their pets' lives. As in the human market, organic pet foods need to meet certain criteria to prove that the ingredients in the food are grown organically before they can bear the label.

Food intended for human consumption meets different standards than food intended for animal consumption. More and more, pet owners want to know that the quality of their pets' food is just as good as their own. They like the fact that they could sit down and eat the same food their pets eat. Some pet owners go the extra step and make their own food for their dogs. (See below.) But these human-quality foods are an easy alternative to homemade.

Whether they're organic or human-grade, these foods are generally more expensive. They cost more to make, and they're often made by smaller companies that don't produce the same quantities as larger manufacturers. These diets can generally be found at pet-specialty retailers.

How to Read the Label

No doubt you read the labels on foods you eat. They contain basic information about the item, including its calories, nutrient content, and ingredients. Dog food labels are no different.

Pet foods are regulated by the Food Standards Agency and must contain

It's important that the size of your Yorkie's food be small enough for his tiny mouth.

certain information on their labels. The information includes the feeding instructions, the guaranteed analysis, the ingredients, the nutritional adequacy statement, and contact information.

The first part of the label is the feeding instructions. This section gives guidelines for how much to feed your Yorkie based on his weight. If it's a diet formulated for puppies, it will give feeding instructions based on age, too. Sometimes, it will include information about when and how often you should feed your dog.

The guaranteed analysis breaks down by percentage what nutrients are in the food. It lists minimum levels of crude protein and crude fat, and maximum levels of crude fibre and moisture. It also includes percentages or measurements of additives, vitamins, and minerals discussed earlier.

The label also includes the ingredients in descending order. Often, a form of protein appears first in line, followed by grains, fats, additives, and preservatives.

The nutritional adequacy statement says whether the food provides complete balanced nutrition for a dog based on nutritional levels established by the Pet Food Manufacturers Association. The statement also provides a life stage claim, which states the life stage for which the food is intended. Two nutrient profiles for dogs have been developed: growth/lactation and maintenance. All foods must meet at least one of these profiles. Some labels claim the food is intended for all life stages. Those foods provide enough nutrients for an animal's growth and reproduction as well as for maintaining a healthy adult.

Dog food manufacturers also must provide contact information of the manufacturer, packer, or distributor.

SENIOR DOG TIP

Veteran Diets

As Yorkies age, their bodies don't move as they once did. They are less active, and therefore require fewer calories. If they eat the same amount they did when they were young adolescents, they tend to become obese.

Older dogs' systems also tend not to absorb nutrients as they once did. Their bones become softer, their coats lose their luster, and their kidney functions slow down.

Pet food labels often include feeding instructions for older dogs. Some pet foods are designed for the needs of older dogs, and often contain supplements, such as chondroitin and glucosamine, that purportedly ease joint pain. Others may include added vitamins and minerals.

Read your dog's food label, and consult your vet for advice. He might have your older Yorkie switch to a veteran formula or take some vitamin supplements. But if his diet is a premium well-balanced blend, your dog is already getting all the nutrition he needs.

A name and address are required; sometimes manufacturers include a free phone number or Web site address, but these are not mandatory.

Armed with this information, you can now examine your Yorkie's food label with confidence. Call the manufacturer if you have questions.

Non-Commercial Foods

In addition to the commercial diets on the market, two non-commercial choices—raw diets and homemade diets—allow Yorkie owners to have more control over what they feed their pets. Commercial diets contain everything the dog needs to thrive, yet some people prefer to prepare their dogs' meals themselves.

Raw Diets

Raw diets are just what you would expect: raw meat and bones that you feed to your dog. Proponents and opponents each have their varying opinions on this type of diet. Some believe the diet improves their pets' skin, coat, and teeth, improving their stamina and vitality. Others caution against E. coli, parasites, and other risks associated with raw meats. These diets are often supplemented by some source of fibre and vitamins to ensure the full range of nutrients.

Some manufacturers have begun selling raw diets at pet stores. Often found in a freezer, these diets are individually packaged to make feeding simple.

the diet? Preparing a homemade or raw diet is just like cooking for another member of the family. The food should be prepared every few days to ensure freshness.

• Do you have the space to store the raw meat or meals? Because these foods do not have preservatives, they need to be stored in the refrigerator or the freezer.

• Do you travel a lot? If so, a diet like this may not be appropriate. Dog sitters or boarding kennels might not be able to make dinner for your dog every night. And if the dog travels with you, you might not have access to the foods or a kitchen.

Homemade Diets

Homemade diets are meals made from scratch. Often fed to finicky dogs or those with food allergies, these diets incorporate whole foods, such as potatoes or rice, and protein sources, such as cooked chicken or beef, that are not packed full of preservatives. Yorkies don't eat a lot, so preparing homemade meals can be relatively simple as long as you include all the nutrients that your Yorkie needs.

Non-commercial Diet Considerations

Before feeding your Yorkie a raw or homemade diet, consider these factors:

• Do you have the time to prepare

• Do you have access to organic meats, or is there a reliable butcher near you?

• Do you know enough about dog nutrition to ensure your Yorkie is getting all the vitamins and minerals he requires?

If you're going to feed your Yorkie this type of diet, first and foremost, visit a vet. Specialist nutritionists may be consulted to help you develop a diet for your Yorkie. You might even want to talk to a conventional and a holistic vet to hear their opinions.

A Yorkie's tolerance to diet changes is fairly strong, but for the health of your dog, consult a veterinary surgeon

Feeding Chart

Age	Times per Day	Amount	Best Food
Puppies (after weaning to 12 weeks old)	Up to four times per day, along with a bowl of dry food left out all day	1/2 to 3/4 cup (151.8 to 340.2 g) total	One designed for growth; higher in protein; softer bites for ease on the gums
Adolescents (3 months to 6 months old)	Three times per day	1/2 to 3/4 cup (151.8 to 340.2 g) total	One designed for growth; higher in protein
Active Adult (those that exercise for up to two hours per day)	Two times per day	1 1/4 cup (567 g) per day	One designed for maintenance.
Sedentary Adults (indoor dogs)	Two times per day	3/4 to 2/3 cup (340.2 to 453.6 g) per day	One designed for maintenance
Veterans (older than 8 years)	Two times per day	3/4 to 2/3 cup (340.2 to 453.6 g) per day	One designed for mature dogs; often has more fibre

before introducing him to raw or homemade meals.

Feeding Requirements

Yorkie puppies and adults have different feeding requirements. They not only need different types of food, but they also have different eating habits.

Young puppies need to eat up to four meals throughout the day to stimulate growth, keep their metabolisms fuelled, and prevent hypoglycaemia, or low blood sugar. Some experts recommend free-feeding puppies, which means leaving dry food out all day and allowing the pup

to eat whenever he feels like it. The free-feeding is then supplemented by regularly scheduled meal times.

Puppies up to 12 weeks old should be fed four times a day in addition to having dry food available. As they get older, the feedings should steadily decrease. From week 13 to week 24, the pups should be fed three times a day. From six months on, your Yorkie should be fed twice a day.

Free-feeding your puppy allows him to eat whenever he is hungry, which can prevent hypoglycaemia. But as the pup gets older and his body learns how to utilise the sugar appropriately, you should stop free-feeding and stick with the twice-a-day routine. If the food is out all day, the adult Yorkie will eat it, and if he's not getting enough exercise, the petite dog will quickly pack on the pounds.

The amount of food you feed your Yorkie will depend on the individual dog. Generally, you'll feed adults 1/3 to 1/2 cup (226.8 to 151.8 g) per meal. Gauge the amounts by how the dog looks. If your Yorkie has a bulging belly, decrease the amount a bit to correct the weight gain.

Obesity

More pets than ever are obese, and Yorkies are no exception. A high calorie intake and a sedentary lifestyle result in an overweight pup. Yorkie adults who eat too much at mealtime, free feed, or enjoy too many treats end up consuming too many calories, and weight gain ensues. And if exercise isn't a part of their daily lifestyle, those extra calories never have chance to be burned off.

If your pet is packing on the pounds, you have two choices. You could simply decrease the amount of food—both his regular diet and treats—that you're feeding your pet. This will lower the amount of calories he is consuming without changing his diet.

Or you could change the diet to a "light" formula. Some people feel that this might not be as healthy as simply feeding less. But just as there are formulas for veteran dogs, there are formulas for overweight dogs. As always, talk to your vet before changing your Yorkie's diet.

Feeding your Yorkie a delicious diet is one of the most important things you'll do for your pet. With so many choices, you'll find a diet your dog is sure to like. Feed him in moderation, offer him plenty of water to wash it down, and exercise him often—this is the best way to ensure a healthy dog.

Table Manners

How can you resist that face? Your Yorkie hops up on your lap while you're eating and looks at you with those dark eyes, begging for a bite. Should you share your snack? It's not a good idea. Human food, though delicious, can be harmful to Yorkies. Besides being too calorie-packed and rich, dogs who get a taste for human food might never go back to dry dog food! Some foods, like chocolate and garlic, are actually poisonous to dogs.

Instead, train your Yorkie to lay down on his bed, play with his toys, and wait for his humans to finish eating. Then he can eat all the dry food he wants—and maybe even a treat or two!

Chapter 4

Looking Good

One of the things that probably drew you to a Yorkshire Terrier was his long, silky coat. Who could resist the layers of flowing human-like hair and the cute top knot tied with a red bow, all framing that adorable face?

Keeping those locks—not to mention his nails, eyes, ears, and teeth—looking their best will take some work. You can expect daily, weekly, and semi-monthly grooming rituals to maintain that stunning appearance. It may sound like a lot of responsibility, but after becoming familiar with the handling, the tools, and the processes, grooming time will be a pleasurable experience for you and your Yorkie, resulting in a strong bond you both will enjoy.

Using a Groomer

Some Yorkie owners choose to take their pet to the groomer for regular shampooing, nail trimming, teeth and ear cleaning. Groomers are professionals who specialise in keeping your dog looking good. Some take classes to perfect cutting techniques, and some compete in grooming shows. These "dog hairdressers" generally have their own premises. Often, you can find a groomer through references from your breeder, veterinary surgeon, friend, or colleague.

In the US, dog spas are another stylish option that has enjoyed growth in the past five years. Yorkie owners can drop their dogs off at the spa for a day of aromatherapy, hair styling, grooming, massage, and more. These are fun upscale options for pampered Yorkie "kids."

If you decide to hire a groomer, inspect the facility first.
- Is it clean?
- Does it smell musty or dirty?

- Do they require vaccinations or health screenings?
- Is there hair all over the floor?
- Is the room temperature warm enough to keep your wet Yorkie comfortable?
- Do you feel confident leaving your baby with this person for several hours?
- What types of tools and equipment does she use?
- Does she stay on top of the product trends?

You should feel extremely comfortable with your groomer. She literally has your dog's life in her hands.

A grooming table can come in handy if you are taking care of your Yorkie's coat on your own.

Even if you rely on a groomer for weekly upkeep, you will still need to perform daily duties to keep your Yorkie looking good between appointments. Let's take a closer look at the different parts that need grooming, why it's important to groom them, how to do it, and how often.

Doing It Yourself

Yorkies can easily be groomed at home. With just a few tools, a little instruction, and a short amount of time each day, you can maintain your Yorkie's coat, keep his nails trimmed, eyes and ears clean, and teeth sparkling.

Many breeders prepare their pups for grooming when they're still very young. They hold them and coddle them, looking at their mouths, their paws, and their eyes and ears. Most likely, by the time your Yorkie met you he was used to being handled.

You can continue the breeder's or previous owner's work by handling your Yorkie every day. Your dog needs to feel comfortable with someone touching his body, inspecting his eyes and ears, tickling his toes, and even rubbing his gums.

Choose a Location

To begin grooming your Yorkie at home, you must first choose a specific location. Choosing one place will teach your dog what to expect and how to behave while you're grooming him. Some people use a countertop, others use a grooming table, which allows them the flexibility to walk around it. Whatever surface you choose,

Create a Grooming Area

When you groom your Yorkie at home, create a grooming area that has all the tools you'll need in one convenient location. Here are some of the items you'll need to have in close proximity:

- A flat surface, such as a countertop or table, that can be cleaned. It should give you easy access to your Yorkie when you're sitting or standing.
- A non-skid pad, either permanent or removable, over the top to ensure your Yorkie's sure footing.
- A sink or a tub with a non-skid pad, and hot and cold water, ideally with a hand-held shower attachment/sprayer.
- A basket or tool kit that contains all the grooming essentials, including the shampoo and conditioner, conditioning spray, comb, brush, scissors, nail clippers, cotton balls, toothbrush and toothpaste, blow dryer, hair ties and ribbons.
- Access to an electrical outlet.
- A stack of clean towels.

always put a non-slip pad or towel on the surface—and *never* leave your Yorkie unattended.

Getting Accustomed to Grooming

If you do choose to purchase a grooming table, let your Yorkie get used to it—allow him to sniff and inspect it for his approval. While your Yorkie is growing accustomed to the table, run your hands over his entire body. Gently give your dog a massage, feeling every bone, muscle, and tendon. Encourage good behaviour by rewarding him with toys and treats. This will not only prepare your dog for grooming rituals, but it will also help you become more aware of how your dog normally feels. If he should develop a lump or injure himself, you'll know right away.

Next, show your Yorkie the grooming tools. You don't need to use them on the dog just yet; have them out and let him inspect these new items. Slowly introduce him to the pin brush, the comb, the toothbrush, and the blow dryer, rewarding him for good behaviour. Soon, your Yorkie will jump for joy when the grooming toolkit comes out!

Grooming Supplies Checklist

Whether you take your Yorkie to the groomer or do it yourself, you'll want to have these tools and supplies available. They can all be found at your local pet shop, online, or through your groomer.

- **Shampoo and conditioner.** There are many on the market, but choose one formulated for a small dog with long hair. Avoid the shampoo-conditioner combos. They may cut bath time in half, but the coat won't be as clean. And you want to do everything you can to preserve that coat!
- **Hair dryer.** You can find many varieties of these, including hands-free standing models. Make sure it has is a low or cool setting, and the quieter, the better.
- **Grooming or conditioning spray.** You'll use this leave-in, spray-on conditioner during your daily brushings. Ask your pet store salesperson or groomer for recommendations.
- **Comb.** If you can afford it, purchase a quality

44

Yorkshire Terriers

It is important to get your Yorkie accustomed to grooming and grooming tools.

metal or stainless steel comb with long teeth. The type with narrow teeth on one side and wider teeth on the other will give you more combing options.

The long coat of the Yorkie is mainly for show dogs; pet owners usually keep their dogs' coats in a shorter cut.

- **Pin brush**. These are rubber-backed brushes with fine pins. Sometimes, the pins have small rubber balls on the ends, which can pull at the hair and damage the coat. Choose one without the rubber balls, if possible.

- **Dematter**. Eventually, you will need this device to pull out mats from your Yorkie's coat. This brush has several curved blades that are sharp on one side.

- **Scissors**. Small scissors are used for trimming the hair around your Yorkie's ears, the bottom of the

FAMILY-FRIENDLY TIP

A Child's Brush with Grooming

Involving a child in the grooming regime is as simple as handing him or her a pin brush. For example, when 10-year-old Sara helps her mother groom their Yorkie, she patiently waits while her mother works out all the tangles and knots in the dog's coat. She watches her mother comb through each section of the pup's hair, making sure each strand is clean and conditioned. Only then does Sara get to brush her dog's coat.

Sara's mother taught her to be gentle and not pull the coat or the skin too hard. Sara has learned how to care for the dog, and the dog benefits from bonding with her.

A child can also help with shampooing the dog. He or she can massage the dog while washing the dog's coat. After you rinse out the shampoo, he or she can help with the conditioner, too.

If the child is old enough, consider enlisting his or her help when trimming your Yorkie's nails. You'll need someone to hold your dog, and who better than your child?

By giving your children grooming responsibilities, they'll develop a better understanding of pet ownership and be able to appreciate the joys and challenges it involves.

feet, and the anus. Select small-blade scissors that fit your hand comfortably.

- **Nail clippers.** The two basic types are the scissor cut and the guillotine cut. Purchase whichever you're most comfortable with.
- **Styptic powder.** Styptic powder, which stops the flow of blood, is good to have on hand for unexpected nail-trimming accidents.
- **Cotton-wool balls.** You'll use these for cleaning out your Yorkie's ears and around his eyes.
- **Toothbrush and dog toothpaste.** A child's soft toothbrush with some dog-specific toothpaste will keep your Yorkie's teeth tartar-free.

Coat and Skin Care

That long, lustrous Yorkie coat is beautiful, and to keep it looking its best you're going to be doing some daily brushing and semimonthly washing.

The Yorkie is a single-coated breed, which means he has no undercoat to keep him warm. Each silken strand comes from one hair shaft and, just like human hair, the Yorkie's hair grows continually. Oils from sebaceous glands under the skin naturally condition the hair and skin. Too much washing can cause dry, flaky skin and chapping, but daily brushing releases the oils, keeps the skin and coat healthy, and prevents tangles and mats from forming.

The texture of the Yorkie's hair is silky and strong. When brushed daily and kept clean, mats and tangles generally aren't a problem. But if a piece of debris gets caught in that long

often sport the longer cuts, but active Yorkies with busy owners benefit from a shorter cut. Based on your lifestyle and preference, your groomer can help you decide which style is best for you and your dog.

Daily Brushing

No matter the cut, your Yorkie requires daily brushing to keep his coat healthy and mat-free. Yorkies don't shed twice a year like other dogs, and their hair has a tendency to break off during brushing. To prevent this from happening, spray your dog's hair with a conditioning spray before brushing to soften and coat it.

Place your Yorkie on your designated grooming spot. Begin by using a comb and your fingers to gently loosen any tangles. If the tangle is difficult to release, spray it with some extra conditioner and continue working it. Eventually it should loosen, but you may need to cut out stubborn knots. Using small scissors, carefully trim around the mat, being careful not to pull at your Yorkie's sensitive skin.

Once the knots and tangles are out, continue combing through your Yorkie's hair in sections. Portion off a section of the coat with your hand and comb through it, starting at the tip and working up to the root, until you can comb through the section with no resistance. Then move to the next section. You can start at the front or the back, but don't forget your dog's

coat and it's neglected for any length of time, it could turn into a Yorkie dreadlock. After romping in the park or playing in some dewy grass, check your Yorkie's coat for debris and comb it out as soon as possible.

Yorkie owners keep their pets' hair trimmed in several styles: the quintessential Yorkie cut, which features long flowing hair; a puppy cut, which is short all over; or a modified Schnauzer or Westie cut, which is somewhere in-between. Indoor Yorkies, show dogs, or more sedentary dogs whose owners have time to groom

> *Be careful not to get water in your Yorkie's ears when you bathe him.*

abdomen and chest hair! They're most vulnerable to tangles and mats.

After you can comb smoothly through the coat, part it down the middle of your dog's back and brush him with a pin brush from root to tip, being careful not to scrape the skin. This stimulates oil production, encourages growth, and removes any loose hairs. A final comb through will smooth the coat and make it glisten. Finishing sprays will keep the coat in place and add that extra shine.

Brushing around your Yorkie's face is also a daily chore. You'll want to comb out and replace your pet's top knot, clean around his eyes, and remove the food and other debris from his beard.

The Top Knot

The top knot is essential for this breed—it keeps the Yorkie's hair out of his eyes. A top knot is the ponytail on top of the Yorkie's head, usually held together by a bow or barrette. To achieve this look, gather all the hair from the forehead and gently comb it out. Use a covered rubber band to gather the hair together, being careful not to pull it too tight. If the hair is short, pull the hair all the way through, but if the hair is long, pull only part of the hair through to form a folded-over knot. Finish it off with a bow or barrette fastened over the rubber band (red is a popular colour choice—it seems to compliment the colour of the coat).

The Eyes

Sometimes, mucous will accumulate around the Yorkie's eyes. This can easily be cleaned by softening it and removing it with a damp cloth or cotton-wool ball. Then, carefully comb through the moistened hair with a fine-toothed comb.

The Beard

The beard, which can grow very long, includes the area below his eyes down to his muzzle and chin. It gets wet every time your Yorkie drinks, and it holds bits of food after each meal. Outdoor Yorkies who sniff, dig, and hunt will add dirt to the mix. Because the beard picks up so much debris, daily brushing—and sometimes washing—is essential.

Follow the same combing technique used on the dog's body: Work out the knots in the beard, and comb from the tip to the root until the hair combs through with no resistance. Part the hair down the middle of his muzzle.

You'll need to wash the beard if the food and debris won't comb out. Some Yorkie owners wipe their dogs' faces after every meal, ensuring those little bits of food won't turn into messy mats. Other Yorkie owners keep the beard trimmed to 3 or 4 inches (7.6 to 10.2 cm) to help cut down on debris collection.

Weekly Bathing

Depending on their activity level, Yorkies require weekly or semimonthly baths. Any more than that will dry out your Yorkie's skin and cause dandruff and brittle hair.

Before bath time, gather all the gear you'll need to wash, dry, and comb out your dog. You'll need shampoo, conditioner, a couple of fluffy towels, cotton-wool balls, a comb, a pin brush, and a hair dryer.

First, brush out your Yorkie's coat thoroughly before bathing him. Tangles and mats will only tighten up and worsen in the tub.

Next, prepare the bathing area. Many Yorkie owners use the kitchen or bathroom sink to bathe their tiny pets, while others use the bathtub. Place a non-slip mat on the base of the sink and place your shampoo, conditioner, and towels nearby. Gently plug your Yorkie's ears with cotton-wool balls and put him in the sink.

SENIOR DOG TIP

Grooming the Older Dog

Older Yorkies require just as much grooming as younger dogs. Veterans enjoy being fussed over, talked to, and coddled. They enjoy the attention and look forward to grooming as a time to relax and bond with their owners.

While massaging and brushing your older Yorkie, diligently check for lumps. Look for swelling or tender spots that could signal a problem.

As Yorkies age, their sebaceous glands produce less natural oils, so their coats may lose their lustre. Regular bathing, conditioning, and brushing will keep their skin and coat healthy. Their nails will need trimming, too. They grow more quickly when the dogs are older, and longer nails make mobility even more difficult.

Dental health is increasingly important as your Yorkie ages. Continue brushing your pet's teeth and checking for signs of infection or gingivitis. You want your older dog to be able to enjoy his food to the very end!

49

Trouble Spots

It's inevitable. Your Yorkie drags his flowing locks through some sticky burrs and twigs, or picks up a bright piece of bubble gum in his hair. What do you do?

Burrs, twigs, and other hair-tanglers: Those little pieces of nature are sure to cause knots and mats in your Yorkie's silky coat. Comb them out as soon as possible with a fine-toothed comb. Stubborn pieces can be coaxed out using some conditioning spray. In a worst-case scenario, you might have to cut out the knots.

Bubble gum: What a sticky mess! Before pulling out the scissors, rub the gum with ice cubes and try to break it out. If that doesn't work, use some conditioner, vegetable oil, or peanut butter to pull it out. If none of those methods work, it's time to get the scissors.

Paint: All paint is toxic, so you'll need to remove it immediately and not let your Yorkie ingest any of it. Latex paint is water-soluble, so it will rinse out with water. Oil-based paint will necessitate a trim. Never use turpentine or any solvent on your Yorkie's coat.

With lukewarm water, rinse your dog's head and body, being careful not to get water in his ears. A pull-out nozzle or hand sprayer attached to the tap makes this job easy. Once he's thoroughly wet, turn off the water.

Using a quarter-size drop of shampoo, wash and massage your Yorkshire Terrier's coat and skin, including his ears, underside, and rear. Do not get the shampoo near his eyes. Rinse the soap out completely, working from his head down his back and underneath his body. Then apply the conditioner according to the manufacturer's instructions. Let the conditoner soak in, and then rinse thoroughly.

Drying

Don't let your Yorkie run around wet to air dry after bath time; he could catch a cold. Instead, wrap your clean dog in a big fluffy towel to soak up the excess water. Cuddle and warm him for a few minutes. Then move over to the hair dryer.

Lay your Yorkie on your grooming table and begin blow drying his hair. Use the lowest setting possible, and keep the dryer at least 8 inches (20.3 cm) from your dog's body to prevent scalding. With the dryer in one hand and a pin brush in the other, dry your dog's abdomen, chest, and leg areas while brushing his hair. Then stand him up and brush and dry the outer layers of the coat from the roots to the tips.

Finish your Yorkie's bathing session by combing him out, parting his coat down the middle, and securing his top knot. Now he's ready for some nail, dental, and ear care.

Nail Care

Nail trimming is another grooming ritual that should be done weekly. You know your Yorkie's nails have grown too long if you hear click-clicking when he walks across the floor! An ideal time to trim your Yorkie's nails is after his bath when his nails are softened from the warm water—but any time will do.

Like all dogs, your Yorkie's toenails grow continually and need to be trimmed to keep them at a healthy length. If they grow too long past the pads of the feet, they could curve inward and cut into the pad. Long nails can also cause the dog to lose traction, as they could prevent his pads from hitting the ground. They can tear upholstery, snag clothing, and cause scratches, too.

You can choose from several types of nail trimmers at your local pet store. Whichever style you choose, select the smallest size for your Yorkie's tiny nails.

The Quick

Most Yorkie toenails are black. This makes it difficult to see the quick, which is the vein inside the nail. Clipping the quick is painful and can cause your Yorkie's nail to bleed. To find the quick, use a flashlight or look at your dog's nails outside—you should be able to see the opaque portion in the centre base of the nail—that's the quick.

How to Trim Your Yorkie's Nails

When you trim your dog's nails for the first few times, enlist the help of another person to steady your Yorkie. Having an extra set of hands will be very helpful when your dog starts squirming!

You can position your Yorkie in a number of ways: held against your chest, standing on a table or other non-skid spot, or laying on his back. Choose the position that's most comfortable for you.

With the dog held securely in place by your assistant, hold the trimmers with your dominant

When trimming nails, be careful not to cut the quick.

hand and the dog's paw with the other. Start with one toenail. Gently press your index finger and your thumb on the toe, which extends the nail and prevents it from retracting. Only clip off the portion of the nail that's curving downward. If you're nervous about cutting the quick, clip only the very tip and have some styptic powder nearby just in case. With time, trimming your Yorkie's nails will become second nature to you both.

In addition to trimming your Yorkie's nails, you'll also want to trim the hair that grows between the dog's pads and toes. This hair can pick up dirt and debris, causing mats to form. Simply trim the hair carefully with a pair of small scissors.

Dental Care

Dental hygiene is an extremely important part of your Yorkie's grooming routine. Bacteria buildup from poor oral health has been linked to infection and disease in dogs' major organs, including their hearts, livers, and kidneys.

Oral health is especially important for Yorkies and other toy breeds. Because of their size, they have smaller jaws and weaker gums. Tartar builds up quickly, resulting in plaque, gingivitis, and bad breath. The dog's gums become swollen and irritated, and in extreme instances bleed and fill with pus. If left untreated, periodontal

Yorkshire Terriers

The Expert Knows

Those Special Moments

Grooming your Yorkie offers a wonderful opportunity to bond with your pet. These daily brushings allow you to spend quality time with your dog—you can massage him and shower him with attention. Often, your dog is calm and relaxed from gentle, careful grooming. Remember you are caring for a member of your family, so treasure these special moments with your Yorkie.

disease could set in, and the dog may need to have his teeth pulled. All of this can be prevented by establishing and maintaining good dental care habits.

Your Yorkie's teeth should be brushed several times per week with a child's soft toothbrush and toothpaste designed especially for dogs, not for humans. Human toothpaste is not safe for your Yorkie, and he probably won't like the taste. The brushing will wash away the tartar and break up the plaque. If your Yorkie doesn't like the toothbrush, try massaging his teeth and gums with dog toothpaste on your finger to get it used to the procedure.

Use a circular motion when brushing your dog's teeth, just as you use on your own teeth. Clean the outside and the inside of the teeth, and don't miss those teeth in the back of the mouth—plaque and tartar tend to accumulate there the most. At first, this toothbrushing ritual can be done with your Yorkie sitting in your lap. When he grows accustomed to the routine, brush his teeth on the designated grooming table.

In addition to brushing, offer your Yorkie treats designed to break down tartar and plaque. Several are available from pet supply stores; ask your retailer or vet for recommendations. Feeding your Yorkie dry food can also break down plaque that builds up on the teeth, but there is no substitute for actually brushing your little dog's teeth.

Yorkies who aren't eating, drinking, or playing with their favourite chew toys may be suffering from gum disease. Look at your dog's teeth and gums and call your veterinary surgeon if you suspect something is wrong. In some cases, a vet must anaesthetise the dog to clean a neglected mouth. Like any surgery, this procedure has risks. Avoid it by maintaining your Yorkie's oral health and visiting your vet regularly for teeth-cleaning sessions.

Ear Care

Along with your tooth-brushing routine, add ear cleaning to the list. A Yorkie's ears stand erect, which leaves them prone to dirt, grime, and even ear mites. When they play in the garden or meet friends at the park, their ears are vulnerable to all sorts of debris. Cleaning your dog's ears several times a week will keep them healthy.

Like your Yorkie's other grooming regimes, ear care will take some getting used to. He might not like to have his ears handled at first. Work with your Yorkie until he is comfortable with you touching, looking in his ears, and cleaning them.

Start by inspecting your Yorkie's ears. Gently hold the edge of his ear and check for wax, discharge, odour, or signs of ear mites. A moderate amount of wax is normal, but any discharge or odour could signal other problems, such as an infection. Monitor the situation, and consult your vet if it persists.

Your Yorkie may end up becoming your best accessory!

Grooming time offers a perfect opportunity to give your Yorkie a health check. Inspecting your dog daily for abrasions, lumps, or sore spots will catch potential emergencies early on. Here are some things to check for:

- Start with his face. Look at his eyes, nose, and ears. Do you see any abnormal discharge? Do his eyes sparkle or are they dull and listless? Is his nose cold and damp? How do his ears look? Do they stand erect? Are they clean, or has your Yorkie been scratching at them?

- Next, look at his teeth. As mentioned in the dental health section, a Yorkie's teeth are prone to plaque and tartar buildup, and gingivitis. Do his gums look pink and healthy? Or do they look red and irritated? Has he stopped eating, drinking, or playing with his favourite chew toy? Does he have bad breath? These may be signs of an infection.

- As you massage your Yorkie's body, touch every part and feel for lumps, abrasions, or sore spots. Does your dog relax and enjoy the body rub, or does he flinch when you touch certain parts of his body? If so, consult your vet.

- Finally, check your Yorkie's legs and feet. Look at his legs and his ankles. Handle each foot and each toe. Do the nails extend and retract properly? Is it time for a toenail clipping again?

Doing these mini health checks at least once a week will help you catch any problems early. If you should see something abnormal, contact your vet. It could be a sign of something serious.

Next, using a cotton-wool ball moistened with ear-cleaning solution, wipe the inside of the ear, getting inside all the folds and creases. Use a fresh cotton-wool ball for the other ear. Make sure the ears are thoroughly dried with a clean cotton-wool ball. If possible, cotton buds should be avoided as they can damage the inner ear if used incorrectly. If you see some dark brown or black debris on the cotton-wool ball, your Yorkie might have ear mites, which thrive on ear wax and other debris in the ear canal. Continue to wipe until the cotton-wool ball comes out clean, and do it daily. Shaking heads or scratching at the ears are also signs of possible ear mites. If it persists, talk to your vet about over-the-counter or prescription ear mite remedies.

There are plenty of fashionable accessories for your Yorkie.

Attire and Accessories

Your Yorkie looks good, smells good, and his teeth are sparkling clean. Now all he needs is some dandy duds to wear.

The quintessential Yorkie look usually includes a ribbon or a barrette with a bright red or orange bow on top of his head. But you don't have to stop there—in most pet stores today, you'll find a range of clothing designed especially for dogs. From T-shirts and costumes to designer jackets and booties, your Yorkie can wear just about any outfit to fit his mood.

Typically, Yorkies wear a size extra small. When you're considering a piece of clothing for your dog, take a look at the cut of the attire. It should look like it would fit a dog, not miniaturised clothing for people. The arm holes need to be in the front, not on the sides.

Also take a look at how it fits. It should be adjustable and have some give in areas around the neck, arms, and legs.

Some dog clothing is functional. If it's raining, a slicker will keep your dog warm and dry. If you're going boating with your Yorkie, a floatation jacket will make sure your dog is safe and fashionable. If you're going to a costume party, that bumble bee outfit will certainly create a buzz. Some clothing is purely for the dog owner's benefit. You can decide whether you'll dress your Yorkie in trendy fashions, but whatever you choose make sure it is comfortable.

Chapter 5

Feeling Good

As independent and self-assured as they are, Yorkies can't take care of themselves, especially when it comes to their health. One of the first things you'll need to do as a responsible dog owner is establish a relationship with a vet you trust—someone with whom you'll feel comfortable asking questions, sharing concerns, and calling should the unthinkable happen. You'll be working together toward the goal of ensuring a long and healthy life for your beloved Yorkie.

Finding a Vet

Your vet's job is to keep your Yorkie healthy and protected against disease. He or she will conduct annual screenings and suggest preventive care to ensure your Yorkie will live a long life. He or she will also vaccinate your Yorkie against common diseases, perform treatments should something happen, prescribe remedies, and continue a dialogue with you to address any questions or concerns you may have. Next to you, the vet will become your dog's best friend.

Vets can be found in the phonebook, and from referrals from friends and family. Often, the best referrals come from your breeder or your local training or breed club. The chances are good that vets recommended from these sources have treated many Yorkies. They understand the challenges this toy breed can face and can recommend specific treatments for your dog.

Licensing

Veterinary surgeons are registered by the British Veterinary Association. They complete many years of training and pass rigorous examinations. Specialists, such as behavioural or nutritional specialists, undergo even more training and choose to focus on a particular area of expertise.

Choosing a Surgery

Choosing the right veterinary surgery or hospital for your Yorkie will depend on many criteria that only you can decide. What equipment do they have

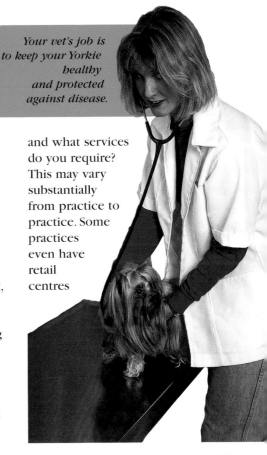

Your vet's job is to keep your Yorkie healthy and protected against disease.

and what services do you require? This may vary substantially from practice to practice. Some practices even have retail centres that allow for one-stop shopping. What level of vet-patient familiarity do you want? In some clinics, you can see the same vet each time you visit; in others, you may not have a choice.

Some other factors to consider include the clinic's proximity to your home, whether they operate an appointment system, and provision of emergency care.

To determine what is right for you, narrow down your selections and visit each one. You may need to schedule a consultation or appointment to fit into the vet's schedule and pay a fee for the visit—but it will give you the opportunity to tour the surgery, meet the staff, and talk to the vet.

When you're there, inspect the surgery for cleanliness and organisation. Note the temperament of the office staff. Be prepared to ask the vet questions, such as the clinic's area of expertise, how long they've been in practice, and whether they offer any alternative therapies. Do they speak to you in a way you'll understand? If you're not comfortable with the vet or the surgery, your dog won't be either.

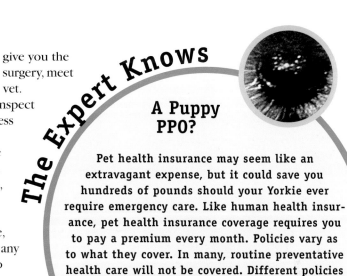

The Expert Knows

A Puppy PPO?

Pet health insurance may seem like an extravagant expense, but it could save you hundreds of pounds should your Yorkie ever require emergency care. Like human health insurance, pet health insurance coverage requires you to pay a premium every month. Policies vary as to what they cover. In many, routine preventative health care will not be covered. Different policies offer different benefits, so be sure to look at all the options before choosing one for your Yorkshire Terrier.

Your Yorkie's First Vet Visit

Your vet will want to see your Yorkie within 48 to 72 hours of arriving at his new home. Most breeders and rescue organisations require that you have your dog checked by a vet soon after purchase or adoption to be sure there are no health problems.

Arrive early to your appointment and bring the documents that came with your Yorkie. They contain important information the doctor needs, such as any vaccinations and tests already performed on your pet. Plan to fill out some preliminary paperwork that lists your dog's vital statistics, activity level, previous health problems (if any), and other pets you may have. You may need to bring a fresh stool sample so your vet can check it for internal parasites.

You'll probably be escorted around the surgery by a veterinary nurse. These trained professionals will weigh your Yorkie, take his temperature, and ask questions about the reason for your visit.

During the physical examination, the vet will conduct an overall health screening to look for potential health problems. He or she will listen to your pup's heart and lungs; feel his abdomen, muscles and joints; inspect his mouth, teeth, and gums; look into his eyes, ears, and nose; and look at your Yorkie's coat. The vet will look for anything out of the ordinary and watch the dog's reaction when handled. The vet will also look for congenital problems, which are health problems an animal is born with.

Feeling Good

The vet will ask you questions about the dog's behaviour. He or she will want to know your Yorkie's eating and defaecating habits, and activity level. If you have witnessed anything out of the ordinary, be sure to tell the vet. Now is the time to ask any questions you may have,

such as what and how much your Yorkie should be eating, any special health problems Yorkies could have, and when your dog should be spayed or castrated. This is the time to establish a comfortable dialogue with your vet.

Annual Visits

This first visit is just the beginning of many regular appointments to come. Annual visits, just like annual check-ups for humans, are a preventive step that ensures continued health. These appointments allow the vet to catch problems early before they turn into life-threatening situations.

During an annual check-up, your vet will conduct an examination similar to your Yorkie's first visit. He or she will examine your dog's overall health, check for any changes, and ask you questions about his behaviour. Your vet will check your dog's vital organs, and look at his eyes, ears, nose, and mouth, as well as feel his body for tumours or sore spots.

If everything checks out, you won't need to visit the vet again for another year. But if something looks amiss, your vet might recommend labouratory work or x-rays. The surgery staff will call with test results as soon as they are available.

Vaccinations

After examining your dog and reviewing his medical records, your vet may decide to vaccinate

Dirty Business

During your Yorkie's check-up, you may need to deliver a fresh stool sample to your vet so it can be examined for things like internal parasites.

Collecting the sample isn't as difficult—or disgusting—as it sounds. It will need to be fresh, so a few hours before your appointment, follow your dog outside with a sealable sandwich bag and a leftover food container with a tight-fitting lid. Turn the plastic bag inside out over your hand and pick up the fresh faeces. Turn the plastic bag back around the sample, seal it, place it in the container, and close the lid. Label it with your name, your dog's name, and the date the sample was taken.

your Yorkie against a range of viruses and bacteria to which dogs are susceptible. If your Yorkie already started his vaccinations, he may need booster shots. Based on recent research that suggests yearly booster shots may be damaging to dogs' immune systems, booster protocols are changing. Some vets give boosters every 18 months, while some veterinary schools recommend that they be given every 36 months. Talk to your vet about his suggested booster schedule and whether he is concerned about the frequency of booster shots.

Dogs face a range of communicable diseases today, but they can be prevented with vaccinations. There are seven diseases against which dogs are usually vaccinated. Whether your vet inoculates against all of them depends on where you live and what viruses are prevalent. Also, if you travel or are planning to travel with your dog, be sure to let your vet know so he or she can vaccinate appropriately.

Here are the most common diseases and what they do:

Distemper. Distemper is a contagious viral disease that causes symptoms resembling a bad cold with a fever. It can include runny nose and eyes, and an upset stomach that could lead to vomiting and diarrhoea. Many infected animals exhibit neurological symptoms. An incurable and deadly disease, distemper is passed through exposure to the saliva, urine, and faeces of foxes and other dogs. Young pups and veteran dogs are most vulnerable to distemper.

Parvovirus. Another deadly virus, parvo attacks the inner lining of a dog's intestines. It causes bloody diarrhoea that has a distinctive smell. Symptoms also include depression, loss of appetite, vomiting, and collapse. As this virus replicates very quickly, prompt medical attention is needed should your Yorkie exhibit

61

Feeling Good

No Unwanted Puppies!

Dogs reach sexual maturity between the ages of 6 to 9 months old, at which time they are capable of reproducing. To prevent unwanted puppies you can have your vet perform a simple surgery on your Yorkie.

Females are spayed. This process involves an ovariohysterectomy, where the ovaries and uterus are removed surgically. The female will be out of sorts for a few days, but she'll be back to her old self in no time. Not only does this procedure prevent unwanted puppies, it also will protect her from ovarian cancer, mammary gland cancer, and decrease the incidence of female aggression.

Males are neutered—their testicles are removed through a small incision just in front of the scrotum. Like the female, the male will be less social for a few days, but he'll be back to normal within a few days. Added benefits of neutering include less marking and leg lifting, less aggression, and protection from testicular cancer.

any of these signs. The vaccination is usually effective.

Hepatitis. Spread through contact with other dogs' saliva, mucous, urine, or faeces, hepatitis affects the liver and kidneys. It causes depression, vomiting, abdominal pain, fever, and jaundice. The mortality rate is high, but vaccination prevents the disease.

Leptospirosis. A highly contagious bacteria that is passed through the urine of infected dogs, rats, and wildlife, leptospirosis attacks the animal's kidneys, causing kidney failure. Symptoms include fever, appetite loss, possible diarrhoea, and jaundice. Vaccinations usually prevent the disease, though the bacteria does appear in different forms,

and the vaccine may not protect against all of them.

Coronavirus. Rarely fatal for adult dogs but deadly to puppies, coronavirus causes a loose watery stool and vomiting.

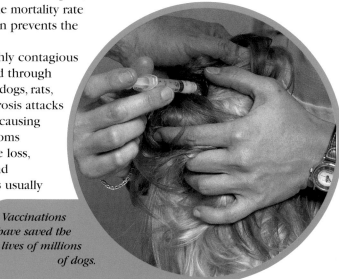

Vaccinations have saved the lives of millions of dogs.

Dehydration from the diarrhoea and vomiting endangers the puppies. The virus is spread through the stool.

Kennel cough. Adenovirus, parainfluenza, and bordatella all refer to a condition known as kennel cough or canine cough. They are rarely deadly, but they do cause significant coughing, sneezing, and hacking, sometimes with nasal discharge and fever. Severe cases may progress to pneumonia. Symptoms may last from several days to several weeks. This condition is very contagious—some forms can be vaccinated against. Dogs that frequent kennels, training classes, groomers, parks, or other public facilities should be vaccinated routinely.

Rabies. Carried in the saliva of infected wildlife and transmitted through bites or abrasions, rabies attacks the nerve tissue and causes paralysis and death. It is always fatal. In the UK, proof of rabies vaccination is required only if you plan to travel abroad.

Parasites

Vaccinations prevent certain viruses and bacteria from afflicting your Yorkie, but he is still susceptible to other medical problems, including external and internal parasites, infections, and accidents.

External Parasites

Fleas and ticks are not fun on your dog—or in your house! These parasites live off your pet's blood. They spread disease, including tapeworms (an internal parasite), and Lyme disease.

Thankfully, these pests can be controlled so you and your pet can enjoy the great outdoors together.

Fleas

Fleas are small crescent-shaped insects that suck the blood from your Yorkie. With their six legs and huge

FAMILY-FRIENDLY TIP

Young Vets

Sara enjoyed going to see the vet with her Yorkie, Ruby. She was there the first time the vet examined her dog. He gave the 10-year-old girl a canine anatomy lesson and let her listen to her dog's heart through the stethoscope. The visit fostered Sara's interest in her dog's health. Now, she looks forward to coming along every time Ruby goes to see the vet.

Children often accompany their mother or father when they take their dog to the vet. As long as the surgery approves, these field trips offer children a mind-opening opportunity to see pet health care up close and personal. Who knows? Perhaps your child could become a vet some day!

Feeling Good

abdomen, fleas can jump surprisingly far in proportion to their size. Their bite causes allergic reactions in dogs and their humans, causing itching, discomfort, and misery!

In large numbers—especially on a little dog like your Yorkie—fleas can cause anaemia and severe allergic reactions that could lead to open sores and possibly a secondary infection.

Fleas also spread internal parasites, such as tapeworms. When a dog swallows a tapeworm-infected flea he then becomes infested with tapeworm. In the past, fleas carried bubonic plague—they are a more than a nuisance, they are a real threat.

Luckily for your Yorkie, more flea-control options exist now than ever before.

- Topical treatments. These treatments are applied to the pup's skin between the shoulder blades. The product moves down the dog's skin and is absorbed into his system. The flea is killed either when it bites the animal or when its reproduction cycle is altered.
- Systemic treatments. These treatments include pills that the dog swallows. When the flea bites the dog, the chemical in the pill is transmitted to the flea, which prevents the flea's eggs from developing, so the population dies off.
- Insect growth regulators (IGRs). IGRs stop the immature flea from maturing and prevent it

from reproducing, so the population ceases to exist.

In addition to treating the dog, you will also need to treat your house and garden for complete flea eradication. The fleas will repopulate if any one of the three is neglected. Treat both the garden and the house with a spray that contains an IGR.

If you prefer to go natural with your external parasite control, several plant-based flea control products are available over the counter. Some of the more popular ones include pyrethrins, which are derived from chrysanthemums, and citrus-based derivatives. They both work to knock down the flea population, but they do little to eradicate an infestation.

Ticks

Ticks are eight-legged bloodsuckers that latch on, embed their head into your pet's skin, and suck

Check your Yorkie for fleas and ticks after he's been outside.

until they become engorged with blood.

Ticks carry blood-transmitted diseases. Depending on where you live, these can include Lyme disease. Lyme disease is characterised by a fever, joint pain, and neurological problems. Although this disease is comparatively uncommon in the UK, it is beginning to occur more frequently. Some flea-control products also deter ticks, but the best thing to do is check your Yorkie after romps in tick-infested areas. During the spring and summer, inspect your dog daily, paying close attention to the areas behind the ears, in the armpit area under the front legs, and around the neck.

If you do find a tick on your pet, you should remove it. Using tweezers to grab hold of the tick as close to the skin as possible, and pull gently but firmly with a twisting motion. Put a little antibiotic ointment on the wound where the tick was embedded.

Most pet owners will have to deal with parasites.

Mange Mites

Mange is caused by tiny microscopic mites that live on your dog. They come in two varieties: sarcoptic mange, which is contagious to people and other pets; and demodectic mange, which is not contagious. Your vet will need to do a skin scraping to determine which variety is plaguing your dog.

Dogs suffering from mange mites may scratch themselves fiercely. Patches of skin look red and scaly, and they may have areas of thinning hair around their eyes, mouth and the fronts of their legs. In more advanced infestations, crusty sores form and ooze, which may lead to secondary infections. Treatment involves bathing in medicated shampoos, steroids to relieve the itching symptoms, and Ivermectin injections.

Ringworm

Ringworm is a contagious fungus that infects the skin and causes a red ring-shaped itchy rash. It spreads by contact from other animals. Ringworm responds well to treatment, but because it is so contagious to people and other animals, the plan must be followed diligently to eradicate the fungus. Treatment for ringworm involves a three-pronged approach: giving your dog a pill that stops the fungus from growing; cleaning the affected area thoroughly and frequently with iodine to kill the fungus on the pet; and keeping your environment

Alternatives

In addition to traditional veterinary care, complementary and alternative health care is an option that you might want to consider for your Yorkie. Some of these alternatives include acupuncture, acupressure, massage, and chiropractic.

Acupuncture and acupressure are ancient Eastern therapies that consist of stimulating precise points by inserting fine needles or applying pressure. Vets are specially trained in practicing this type of therapy. Massage and chiropractic therapy works the animal's muscles and skeletal system to ease pain and speed healing.

Before visiting any of these therapists, consult your vet for recommendations, advice, or further information.

clean using antifungal solutions, such as a 1 to 20 bleach to water ratio.

Internal Parasites

Internal parasites are a part of pet ownership. They aren't pleasant, but they need to be addressed to ensure the health of your pet. Because they're internal, you can't see the damage they're causing! It could take quite some time before the dog exhibits external signs of an internal parasite problem.

Your vet will be able to detect most internal parasites by inspecting your Yorkie's stool sample. It often contains the eggs, dead remains of the parasite, or even the larvae. Your vet will prescribe a treatment, and after it runs its course, you will need to bring in another stool sample to be sure it worked.

Several types of internal parasites affect dogs. Some are more destructive than others. The following parasites are the most common.

Roundworm

Roundworms, which are long white worms, are fairly common in puppies. They can be seen in faeces and vomit, and the eggs are transmitted through the stool. A dog infested with roundworms is thin and might have a dull coat and pot belly. A stool analysis will confirm diagnosis. Good sanitation will prevent the spread of roundworm. Treatment for roundworm infestation involves feeding the dog an oral deworming medication, and repeating it several times to ensure the subsequent generations are destroyed.

Tapeworms

Spread by infected fleas, tapeworms live in an animal's intestine, attach to the wall and absorb nutrients. They grow by creating new segments, which can often be seen around the dog's rectum or in his stool as small rice-like pieces. Your vet can treat the tapeworm by prescribing tablets or giving your dog a series of injections, but a good flea-control programme is the best prevention against tapeworm infestation.

Giardiasis

Commonly passed through wild animals, giardia, a parasitic protozoa, affects humans and animals and causes diarrhoea and lethargy. It is often found in mountain streams, but it can also be found in puddles or stagnant water. Your vet will test for giardia and can prescribe treatment, which consists of giving your pet an oral antibiotic.

Heartworm

Heartworms live in an infected dog's upper heart and arteries, damaging its blood vessel walls. Poor circulation ultimately causes heart failure. The parasite is spread by mosquitoes, and is rarely found in the UK. Adult heartworms produce tiny worms, which circulate throughout the dog's bloodstream. When a mosquito bites a dog, the insect picks up the worms and transmits them to another dog.

Preventive medications are available, and they're very effective. If heartworm is prevalent in your area, your vet will first do a blood test to determine whether your dog is infected. After a clean bill of health, your vet will prescribe the preventative heartworm medication.

Hookworm

Hookworms attach themselves to the small intestine and suck the dog's blood. After detaching and moving to a new location, the wound continues to bleed, causing bloody diarrhoea—often a sign of a hookworm infestation. Like other internal parasites, hookworm eggs are passed through the stool, so good sanitation will prevent their spread. Hookworm treatment involves feeding the dog an oral deworming medication and repeating it one month later. The first treatment destroys the adult worms living in the dog, and the second treatment destroys the next generation.

Whipworm

This internal parasite lives in the large intestine where it feeds on blood. A heavy infestation of whipworms can be fatal, as it can cause severe diarrhoea. Dogs infested with whipworm look anaemic and thin. The whipworm eggs are passed in the faeces and can live in the soil for years, so dogs that dig or eat grass can pick up eggs. If caught early, whipworm can be treated with deworming medications that must be administered over extended periods of time. Because of the long maturation cycle of young worms, a second deworming is needed 75 days after the first one. Additional doses may be necessary, as well.

Breed-Specific Illnesses

Yorkies are tough little dogs, but they are prone to developing several specific physical defects and physiological conditions of which their owners should be aware. Keep an eye on your Yorkie, and if you see any of these conditions develop, let your vet know right away.

Collapsed Trachea

This is a common malady in many toy breeds. Cartilage in the windpipe, or trachea, is weaker than normal and can easily bend or collapse from the slightest pressure, such as pulling on a lead. As the dog ages, the condition worsens and can lead to respiratory problems.

Symptoms of this disorder include strained breathing or a honking cough after exercising, tugging on his collar, or putting any pressure on his windpipe. As the dog ages, the laboured breathing becomes constant, and fluid will begin building in his lungs and obstruct his breathing.

To prevent this or alleviate any existing damage, use a harness instead of a collar to take the pressure off the dog's neck. If your dog exhibits any of these symptoms, talk to your vet about other solutions.

Cushing's Disease

Also known as hyperadrenocorticism,

this disease causes the adrenal glands to overproduce hormones. A Yorkie with Cushing's disease may have poor muscle tone, nervous system disorders, hair loss, excessive thirst and urination, and high blood pressure. This disease often manifests in older dogs. Several treatments involving oral drugs are available, so consult with your vet if your Yorkie exhibits any of these symptoms.

Hydrocephalus

Water on the brain afflicts many small dogs, including Yorkies. A buildup of fluid causes a deterioration and loss of brain tissue. Yorkies with hydrocephalus often have a dome-shaped head and a soft spot that will not close all the way. An ultrasound can confirm a diagnosis.

Signs of this genetic or congenital defect depend on what area of the brain

Yorkies are usually tough, healthy little dogs.

is affected, and can include blindness, trouble learning certain tasks, seizures, or sleepiness. Signs usually appear before the dog's first birthday.

Vets often treat this condition surgically by running a shunt from the brain to the abdomen where the fluid can be reabsorbed into the body. Dogs with mild forms of hydrocephalus can lead normal lives, but serious cases are often dire.

Hypoglycaemia

As we learned in the Chapter 4, Yorkies and other small dogs require regular meals to keep their blood sugar normal. If a dog is overly stressed, sick, or his blood sugar becomes too low, he becomes drowsy and disoriented. He could have seizures and eventually slip into a coma.

Typically affecting puppies and very small Yorkies who weigh under 4 pounds (1.8 kg) when fully grown, hypoglycaemia can be immediately corrected with a dose of syrup or honey on the dog's gums. The sugar will be absorbed into his bloodstream and restore his blood sugar level. Emergency medical attention is required if you are unable to revive the dog. Your vet will have to put the dog on intravenous glucose right away.

Proper management involves feeding your Yorkie regularly and leaving dry food out for him all day. Your vet will be able to offer other advice, too.

First Aid Kit

Every home should have a human first aid kit. But should they also have a canine first aid kit? You bet! Here are the basic ingredients of a medical kit made especially for your Yorkie. Be sure to have it on hand, and make sure your dog sitter knows it's around, too!

- Tweezers
- Scissors
- Small nail clippers
- Rectal thermometer
- Tape
- Bandages (butterfly and standard)
- Elastic bandages
- Rolls of gauze
- Gauze pads of varying sizes
- Instant cold compress
- Antiseptic cleansing wipes
- Alcohol pads
- Eye wash
- Hydrogen peroxide
- Styptic powder
- Benadryl tablets
- Iodine
- Antibiotic ointment
- Bottle of water
- Pen and paper
- Old blanket or sheet
- Cotton-wool balls or cotton buds

Feeling Good

Senior Dog Tip

A Little Help

As dogs age, they develop medical conditions that often require your vet's attention. Though regular visits to your vet for geriatric check-ups will keep these ailments under control, it's a good idea to be aware of some of the challenges your older Yorkie may face.

Arthritis: A degenerative bone disease, arthritis causes stiff joints that can cause your Yorkie to move stiffly or struggle as he gets up. Pain relievers prescribed by your vet can help your dog manage the discomfort. Alternative therapies, such as acupuncture and chiropractic procedures can help, too. You'll also want to give your Yorkie an extra-comfortable bed away from cold draughts.

Cancer: One of the most common health problems older dogs can have, cancer involves the abnormal growth of cells damaging normal body functions. It can be treated through radiation, chemotherapy, and surgery, which can be expensive. Check your Yorkie's body for abnormal lumps or sores that do not heal. Growths can be removed and biopsies can be taken to determine whether they are malignant or benign.

Diabetes mellitus: Diabetes is an abnormal increase in blood sugar levels due to an insulin deficiency. Symptoms of diabetes include an increase in water consumption and urination, weight loss, depression, and refusing to eat. If left untreated, diabetes can cause blindness, infections, and death. Your vet can diagnose and treat this disease.

Heart disease: Heart disease is best managed through prevention. A healthy diet and plenty of exercise will keep your Yorkie's heart strong, but older dogs may develop cardiomyopathy, a weakness of the heart muscle. Yorkies with heart disease appear sluggish and weak. They may cough or have a swollen belly. Let your vet know if your Yorkie develops any of these symptoms.

Kidney failure: Kidneys can become injured at any time in a dog's life, and they tend to wear out in old age. Their job is to filter out all the waste product from the blood and control the body's fluids and electrolytes. When the kidneys stop functioning, the body shuts down. If your Yorkie becomes dehydrated, drinks a lot of water, and urinates more than normal, he may have kidney disease. Regular blood tests check for proper kidney function.

Obesity: Because older dogs move a little more slowly than they used to, they tend to put on some weight in their older years. Obesity increases the risk of diabetes, exacerbates pain caused by arthritis, and can put extra strain on vital organs. Cutting down your Yorkie's diet and treats can help manage the weight gain, as can maintaining his regular exercise routine. (Always talk to your vet before changing your Yorkie's diet.)

Legg-Calve-Perthes Disease

Many toy breeds suffer from Legg-Calve-Perthes disease, a genetic disorder that completely disintegrates the head of a dog's thigh bone. It begins in younger dogs, and as they age, arthritis sets in. The pup limps, and as the disease progresses, the older dog won't even put weight on the leg. Surgery is usually recommended for this painful disease.

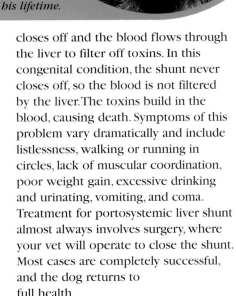

With your vet's help, you can keep your Yorkie healthy and strong for his lifetime.

Luxating Patellas

In some Yorkies, the bones, muscles, and ligaments surrounding their kneecaps, or patellas, are too narrow, weak, or shallow to keep them in place. The kneecaps slip in and out of position when the dog exercises or jumps off the furniture, causing him to hop and skip around until it pops back. The knee can slip inward toward the body or outward. Though this problem can be caused by trauma, often it is a genetic disorder.

Providing ramps or steps down from high places will prevent your Yorkie from leaping off the furniture and dislocating his patella. Surgery can help correct the problem in extreme cases, but your vet can also prescribe anti-inflammatory drugs to help with the pain.

Portosystemic Liver Shunt

When a pup is still a foetus, a shunt diverts the dog's blood around the liver. When the dog is born, the shunt closes off and the blood flows through the liver to filter off toxins. In this congenital condition, the shunt never closes off, so the blood is not filtered by the liver. The toxins build in the blood, causing death. Symptoms of this problem vary dramatically and include listlessness, walking or running in circles, lack of muscular coordination, poor weight gain, excessive drinking and urinating, vomiting, and coma. Treatment for portosystemic liver shunt almost always involves surgery, where your vet will operate to close the shunt. Most cases are completely successful, and the dog returns to full health.

With your vet's help, you can keep your Yorkie healthy and strong for his lifetime. Disease prevention, annual veterinary check-ups, and regular checks of your dog for physiological or neurological changes will hopefully catch problems before they become serious.

Chapter 6

Being Good

Every year, dog owners relinquish millions of dogs to rescue centres because of their pets' bad behaviour. Yet good positive training can help avoid problems before they start. Every dog—from a new Yorkie pup to an adopted older dog—can benefit from training.

Unfortunately, many times an owner's good intentions of proper training fall by the wayside, especially when that new Yorkie pup cutely jumps up on someone's leg or begs for that bite of roast beef. Before long, the Yorkie has assumed control of the house, yapping and biting at strangers or those who come near his food bowl. The frustrated owner sequesters the Yorkie in the kitchen or on the patio, then to the garden, and eventually to the nearest rescue centre.

It doesn't have to be that way.

Behaviour training is about teaching your new Yorkie what actions are allowed and what are forbidden. It also means that you, the owner, will have to be decisive about the things you permit and prohibit. When both you and your dog understand the boundaries, your Yorkie will be able to be a part of your family for a lifetime.

Why All the Fuss?

One of the main reasons to train your Yorkie to obey your commands is to keep him safe. If you're outside and he runs away, a trained dog will return at your command. The untrained Yorkie will keep running and could hurt himself, become lost, or worse. Or, if you're walking through a crowd and you've taught your Yorkie to heel, you know he's not pulling on the lead or getting into trouble.

Another reason to train your Yorkie is to be able to take him out on the town with you, and make him enjoyable for others to be around. This breed is a perfectly portable size, and with a well-trained dog you'll be able to take him to the park, coffee shop, or shopping mall without him barking, running away, or having an accident. People will enjoy coming to your home and playing with your Yorkie if he's not barking, nipping, or growling at them.

Your Yorkie wants nothing more than to please you.

While more and more people think of their dogs as their "children," even kids need to learn rules of behaviour. Your dog should learn proper socialisation—knowing how to act around other people or animals; crate training—teaching your Yorkie where his home base is and how to control his bladder; housetraining—knowing when to relieve himself; and several basic commands, including sit, stay, come, down, and heel. A dog who masters these habits can be considered a well-behaved dog.

Your Yorkie wants nothing more than to please you. He wants to make you happy. Your job is to communicate clearly and firmly what you want him to do through humane training techniques, such as positive reinforcement. You need to make sure your dog knows that you are the leader of the household. The end result will be a happy dog *and* a happy owner.

Different Approaches to Training

Many different training theories and practices exist today. Trainers use different approaches to teach dogs how to behave. Some use a balanced method that incorporates positive reinforcement and correction. Others use a behaviour-driven approach. One aspect that the successful and humane methods have in common is *positive reinforcement*. Positive reinforcement rewards good behaviour with treats, praise, and lots of love. Timing is key when using this approach.

For example, if you're teaching your dog the basic *sit* command, you reward

SENIOR DOG TIP

Too Old for New Tricks?

Young puppies are like blank slates. Nothing has tainted their behaviour yet, so training them is as simple as teaching good manners and reinforcing them through praise and attention.

Older dogs, too, can be taught good manners. They can be taught the *sit, down, stay, come*, and *heel* commands. It might take a little more time and some extra treats here and there, but with patience and good communication, it can be done.

But teaching an older dog can be a challenge. If they've already formed inappropriate habits, those will have to be unlearned before new behaviours can be taught. Sometimes, a behaviour like digging through the rubbish or excessive barking will be too ingrained to be unlearned. In cases like this, a professional trainer can help. He or she can come to your house and evaluate the situation.

Don't give up! Talk to your vet and find a qualified trainer to help. Your veteran Yorkie will thank you for it!

Being Good

him immediately with a treat when he sits correctly. If he doesn't sit correctly, you *don't* say, "Bad dog," and smack him with a newspaper. Instead, you correct the behaviour, gently showing him how to sit correctly, and then ask him to sit again. When he does sit, he is rewarded with a treat and lots of praise.

Behaviour training should start before your Yorkie comes home. Educate yourself by reading books dedicated to positive training and dog behaviour. Or if you are a more visual learner, there are plenty of other types of media on the market, including DVDs and videos, to help you with step-by-step training.

Puppy Class

As soon as your puppy wobbles through the door, training should begin. An 8- to 10-week-old puppy—or a newly adopted adult dog for that matter—can and should learn that biting is not appropriate; that he should sit and stay when his owners are eating; and that he should go outside to relieve himself.

In conjunction with self-educating by using reference materials, consider

enrolling your Yorkie in a training course through your veterinary surgery or through a local dog training club.

Puppy class is for dogs between 10 and 12 weeks old. In most cases, your Yorkie will have to complete at least one round of vaccinations to be allowed to participate. Basic sit, down, stay, and come commands are taught by an instructor who knows the short attention span of a puppy! Not only will your Yorkie learn some basic commands, but he will also have an opportunity to socialise with other dogs.

Basic Training Courses

Basic training courses are for older dogs, 4 months of age or more who have graduated from puppy class but still need some basic obedience instruction. The same commands are taught, and the instructor will also go over some problem behaviours, such as digging, barking, and chewing.

Another option is to hire a private trainer to come to your home. Normally reserved for dogs with severe behaviour problems, private training is done one-on-one and can be individualised to fit you and your Yorkie's needs.

It's never too early to start training—you can begin as early as 8 to 10 weeks old.

Yorkshire Terriers

The Expert Knows

How to Find A Trainer

Taking your Yorkie to a puppy class or dog obedience class should be a fun and educational experience for both of you. It gives your pet a chance to socialise with other dogs and learn how to behave. Often, trainers who run these classes can be found through your veterinary surgery, through your local pet supply store, online, or in the phone book.

Before you settle on one trainer, however, you'll want to visit his or her class and make sure you are comfortable with the training methods. Here are some other things you should look for when you're choosing a trainer for your Yorkie:

1 Observe a class prior to enrolling. The participants should be enjoying themselves and having a successful learning experience. The instructor should be approachable and encouraging, showing courtesy to both the humans and the dogs.

2 A skilled instructor should explain the day's lesson and provide clear instructions through written handouts or demonstrations, give the students plenty of time in class to practice the day's lesson, and assist the students individually with proper techniques.

3 You should be comfortable with the instructor's training tools and methods. They should always be humane and not harmful to the dog or the handler. Hitting, kicking, or any other training device that causes harm or discomfort to the dog should not be used.

4 The trainer should be well-informed about innovations in dog training and behaviour tools and techniques. Ask if the trainer is a member of any educational organisations or associations.

5 Vaccinations should be required before any puppy or dog attends the trainer's class. It protects you and your Yorkshire Terrier's health.

6 Chat with some current clients, if possible, after the class. Find out if they're learning from the instructor and how their dogs are progressing. Good references make a big difference.

7 Ask the trainer if he or she offers some kind of client satisfaction guarantee with the services. Because of variables in dog breeding and temperament, and owner commitment and experience, a trainer cannot and should not guarantee the results of his or her training, but he or she should ensure some type of client satisfaction.

Your Yorkie should learn how to get along with other dogs.

Whether you choose to train your Yorkie yourself, enroll it in puppy class, or enlist the help of a personal trainer, your dog will need to learn the basics of socialising, crate training, housetraining, and obeying specific commands. Let's take a closer look at each one.

Socialising

Socialising your Yorkie is one of the most critical things you can do to ensure a well-mannered dog. As early as possible—by the time your puppy turns 12 weeks old—he should have been exposed to a variety of people, animals, sights, sounds, and circumstances. A well-socialised dog will be confident and brave. He won't be afraid of loud noises or an unfamiliar face, and will get along with other dogs and animals.

Making Introductions

You'll want to introduce your dog to as many people as possible when he's about 9 or 10 weeks old. Let them touch the pup, hold him, pet him, and tickle his toes, but avoid rough games or tug of war. The key is making these experiences positive—choose one well-behaved child, as opposed to a group of loud, rambunctious kids. Try to invite as many people from all ages, genders, ethnicities, and backgrounds as possible to your home to meet your dog. Some trainers recommend that your Yorkie meet as many as 100 people during his first months of life! You want your Yorkie to be familiar with all types of people.

Expose your dog to a variety of sounds, smells, and sights, starting at around 14 weeks old. Put your Yorkie on a lead and take him for a walk through the park. Let him smell the grass, hear the sounds of traffic, and meet people on the street. Introduce him to places you frequent. Carefully open the world to your Yorkie through brief monitored bursts, until he feels comfortable. Week by week, you can introduce more stimuli to your pet.

As soon as your puppy has been inoculated, begin introducing him to other animals, too. Make sure they're well-behaved—then organise play dates, doggy parties, and other supervised meetings between your Yorkie and other dogs. Puppy class is an excellent venue for socialisation. Your pup should also be introduced to other animals, including cats, rabbits, and other pets—always under your watchful eye, of course.

Doggy Language

After awhile, it may seem like you and your Yorkie actually have meaningful conversations. As your closest confidant, your dog knows exactly what you are thinking and feeling. In fact, according to the American Animal Hospital Association's national pet owner's survey, 45 percent of pet owners said their animal listens to them best; their spouses came in second at 30 percent. Besides telling your Yorkie all about your day, you can also communicate through hand gestures and physical behaviours to signal specific things to your pet. Your Yorkie, too, communicates to you through physical gestures. Here are some translations:

Human to Dog
- Raising your horizontal hand, palm up: Sit
- Lowering your horizontal hand, palm down: Down
- Vertical hand with fingers up, palm out: Stay
- Eating first, walking through doors first, tummy rubs: The human is the leader in the house
- Using a stern tone of voice: You're doing something wrong. Stop it.
- Using a happy higher-pitched voice: Let's play!

Dog to Human
- Play bow: When your Yorkie lowers his head and sticks his hips in the air, he wants to play.
- Walking in circles, sniffing: Your Yorkie needs to relieve himself. Take him to his toileting spot, pronto!
- Jumping up and barking: Pay attention to me!
- Climbing up above your shoulders: Vying for the leadership role in the house.

Reducing Fear

Should your Yorkie ever be frightened, resist the temptation to hold him and calm him, which actually encourages fearful behaviour. Instead, show the pup that it's OK to investigate the loud noise. For example, if a book falls to the floor with a loud bang, ask, "What's that?" and walk over to it with your Yorkie on his lead. Touch the book and inspect it. Encourage your Yorkie's confidence and curiosity. If he approaches the book, give the dog lots of praise. Next time, he won't be so skittish.

Expose your Yorkie to various experiences.

To keep your dog well-socialised, you'll need to continue introducing him to new people, circumstances, and pets throughout his life. Regular walks through the neighbourhood or visits to the park will suffice. Take him to your friend's house, the beach, or the pet shop. Continually exposing your Yorkie to various experiences will keep him well-socialised and healthy.

Crate Training

Crate training your Yorkie is another essential step in your dog's behavioural development. You'll use the crate to teach your dog how to control his bladder, as a place to sleep, and as a safe place to relax and chew his favourite toy when he needs some "me time."

Crates can be found at any pet shop or superstore. They come in stainless steel wire, solid plastic, rattan, canvas, or powder-coated metal. They're collapsible, portable, and even airline approved, if required Many of these crates double as carriers, which comes in handy.

Sizing a crate for a Yorkie is easy: You can generally purchase the smallest dog version they have. You might be tempted to give your dog as much space as possible, but all your Yorkie needs—and wants—is enough room to stand up, lie down, stretch out, and turn around. The crate will become his den, a place to feel safe and secure, and too much space defeats this purpose.

Your dog should always associate the crate with a positive experience, not a place for punishment. Place the crate in an area of the house where your family congregates, such as the kitchen or family room, so your Yorkie will not feel lonely. Put some toys and a pad or soft blanket in the crate.

Introducing the Crate

When your Yorkie comes home, you'll want to introduce him to his crate. Talking to the pup with a happy upbeat voice, simply show him the crate, toss a treat inside, and use a command phrase, such as "Go to your kennel." He's bound to go in and explore. Reward him with praise and another treat when he does, but don't shut the door to the crate. Keep repeating this command, action, reward process until your Yorkie associates the command with the treat and, ultimately, the praise. You may need to do this in small steps, but be patient and remember to reward positive behaviour.

Next, you'll want to feed your Yorkie in his kennel. Begin by feeding him near the crate, continuing to associate the crate with a positive experience. With each meal, move the food closer to the crate until he is inside the crate. Place the food towards the back of the kennel and let him go in to eat, leaving the door open. Once your Yorkie sits quietly inside and eats his food, close the door while he eats. At first, open the door immediately after he finishes his meal. But gradually leave the door closed for longer periods until he's comfortable with the door being closed for 10 minutes or so.

If your Yorkie cries or whines to be let out, regress a bit and decrease the time you leave the door closed. Do not let him out until he stops whining, however, because you don't want him to associate whining with getting his way.

Training your Yorkie to stay in his crate for longer periods of time can be done when he feels comfortable staying in his kennel after eating his regular meals. Use the "Go to your kennel" command to get your Yorkie to go inside. Offer a treat and praise to reward good behaviour. Close the door and sit nearby for 10 minutes. Increase the amount of time gradually until your dog sits in his crate for 30 minutes without fussing. After a while, you'll be able to leave him in the crate while you're out for short periods of time, but don't leave him in his crate for more than two or three hours at a time during the day. You'll also want your Yorkie to sleep in his crate at night.

> *There's nothing lovelier than a well-trained Yorkie.*

Being Good

Resist the temptation to let him sleep with you! You could roll over on him during the night and injure him and, in the Yorkie's mind, sleeping on the bed means he is your equal, which could lead to behaviour problems later on. Instead, put the crate in your bedroom and, using the *Go to your kennel* command, instruct your dog to go into his crate. Keep one ear open through the night as your pup will let you know when he needs to relieve himself!

Housetraining

Crate training and housetraining go hand-in-hand. Instinctively, your pup will not eliminate where he eats and sleeps, so he will need to learn bladder and bowel control if he's using the crate as his den. Housetraining includes training your dog to let you know when he needs to relieve himself, where he should go, and how to do it on command. The best time to start housetraining is by 7 to 9 weeks old, when your puppy's physical coordination has been refined.

When your Yorkie comes home, you probably won't know his housetraining habits. He may have been living on sheets of newspaper and allowed to relieve himself anywhere he wanted, or he could understand the concept of going outside. Either way, you'll want to section off an area around the crate, surround it with an x-pen, and lay down some newspaper. This will keep your pup—and his potential accidents—confined. Toy breeds are

notoriously challenging to housetrain, so be patient with your Yorkie while he learns the rules!

Establish a Routine

You don't want your pup to develop a preference for toileting on newspaper, so the first thing you need to do is establish a routine. Your pup's small bladder won't hold much, so you'll need to take him outside frequently: every half hour, after he eats or drinks, and after naps or playtime.

Designate a toilet area outside and take your pup on lead to that area. It could be a patch of grass or soil, a curb, or even a litter tray on your patio (see box, "A Litter Tray for a Dog?"). When he relieves himself, use a voice command, like "Busy" to help him begin associating a command with toileting. Immediately after your Yorkie relieves himself outdoors in the bathroom area, praise him lavishly and give him a treat. Do not wait until he comes inside—by then it's too late, and he won't associate the reward with relieving himself. *Immediately* giving the dog positive reinforcement will let him know what is expected.

Prevention is key to housetraining. Don't give your pup the opportunity to make a mistake. Keep him in your sight at all times by either attaching his lead to your chair or waist or using a baby gate to keep him confined. If you see him start to sniff around or walk in circles, immediately grab the lead and take him outside to him bathroom spot, saying, "Busy." Then praise and give him a treat.

You will need to accompany your pup outside, using the "Busy" command. Going with him is the only way you'll know that he's going to relieve himself and not sniff and play instead. You'll also need to continue praising and rewarding him for relieving himself outside. Eventually, your Yorkie will be able to go on command, which is very useful in the middle of the night or when you're travelling.

Letting You Know

As your puppy ages, he will develop bladder and bowel control, but he will also need to learn how to let you know that he needs to go. When you walk your dog outside to the toilet area, start asking him, "Do you have to be busy?" The pup will learn to associate the question with the "Busy" command, and the praise and reward at the end. Eventually, when you ask your Yorkie if he needs to go, his reaction—either running to the door or standing and staring at you—will be his answer.

Each dog is different, but generally, Yorkies can be considered housetrained by 6 months old, as long as they're not required to hold it too long. Keep in mind the process will take time. Be patient, stick to a schedule, and remember to praise your pup for doing the right thing!

Basic Commands

Obeying basic commands will keep your Yorkie safe and well-behaved at home and in public. By 9 to 12 weeks old, your dog will be focusing on people and be ready to learn

Never punish your Yorkie for housetraining mistakes.

how to sit, lay down, stay, come and heel.

Before you begin, gather some treats such as dehydrated meat or small chunks of cheese. Attach your Yorkie's collar or harness to a short 4-foot (1.2 m) lead and lead him to an area where you'll have plenty of room to work. Plan to dedicate about 20 minutes a day for these training sessions, but practice the commands constantly in your day-to-day activities and encourage your family members to do the same.

Getting Started

Start by teaching your Yorkie to respond to his name when you say it. Standing in front of him, say his name in a fun, upbeat voice. When he looks at you, reward him with lots of praise, toys, and a treat. Practice this for a few days before you begin training, and before long, when your Yorkie hears his name, he will look at you and wait for something to happen.

Sit

The *sit* command teaches your dog to hold still in a sitting position. A very important lesson in self-control, it's probably the first direction your Yorkie will learn. This command is the cornerstone of many to come.

Always using humane training techniques, you can choose from several different methods. One of the easiest is to use a treat as a lure—especially since Yorkies are motivated by food!

Stand in front of your dog. Bend down and hold the treat over his nose.

Say in a firm voice, "Rudy, sit." As you say those words, move the treat up over his head toward his tail. The dog will follow the treat with his eyes and head, which will cause his rear to lower to a seated position. Praise him, saying "Good dog," and reward him immediately with a treat and praise. Do this repeatedly until the dog understands that obeying brings a reward—your praise!

Tiny Treats for Training

Dog treats range from biscuits to rawhides and large pizza-shaped goodies that will keep your Yorkie busy for hours. These types of treats, however, are not designed for training. They're too big and take too long to eat.

When you're training your dog, most experts recommend small chopped up pieces of real meat, such as hot dogs and dehydrated liver or cheese, which can be popped into your dog's mouth. The protein is healthy for your carnivorous pet, and the smaller bites will keep off those extra Yorkie pounds!

Down

The *down* command teaches your Yorkie to lay down and remain in place. You can use this command when you want your Yorkie to lay down on his bed and play with a toy or to stay away from the table when humans are eating.

Begin by telling your dog to sit. Then, holding a treat in front of his nose, say, "Rudy, down," and move the treat down to the floor in front of his paws. As his nose follows the treat and he lays down, praise him and give him the reward. Repeat this process until he's got "down" down.

Stay

The *stay* command, used with both the *sit* and the *down* command, trains your Yorkie to stay in place until you release him. The *sit-stay* command is for shorter periods of time; the *down-stay* command is for longer periods.

Start by facing your dog and telling him to sit. With an open palm facing his nose, say, "Rudy, stay." Slowly stand up, take one step backward and stay there. If your Yorkie stays in place, go back to him after a few seconds and reward him with treats and praise. Gradually increase the time and distance as your Yorkie gets the hand of this command.

If he's fidgeting and coming toward you, enlist the help of a friend or relative. Have them hold your Yorkie's lead gently but firmly after you give the command. Repeat the process until your Yorkie is trained, praising him all the

Small treats are a great training tool for your Yorkie.

time. Continue this training until your dog stays in place for long periods of time.

Come

Teach the *come* command after the *stay* command—it is one of the most important commands to master. Your Yorkie should learn to come to you immediately the first time you call him. Learning to obey this command will keep your dog out of danger.

Luckily, this command is easy to teach. Start with your Yorkie on a fairly

Sara Says Sit

Sara and her Yorkie, Ruby, regularly practice the lessons they learn in puppy class. The 10-year-old girl tells her dog to sit, stay, and heel, and the pup obeys. The dog knows not only to obey the adults, but the kids, too.

At an appropriate age, your child can be involved with your Yorkie's training. Though the child should never be left alone with the dog or be completely responsible for his training, your child can, with supervision, perform the same training techniques you use.

Here are some other ways to get your child involved:

• Include the child in selecting reference materials and DVDs.

• Allow the child to attend puppy class and obedience training classes with you and your dog.

• Under your supervision, have your child practice the *sit, down, stay, come,* and *heel* commands.

Getting your child involved not only solidifies the bond between the child and the dog, but it also communicates to your Yorkie he should be submissive to the child; that the child is higher in social status and should be obeyed.

short lead. Using a treat as a lure, say, "Rudy, come," and walk backwards, which will cause your dog to follow you. Reward and praise him when he reaches you. Continue doing this with a longer and longer lead, even one up to 20 feet (6.1 m) long. Before long, your dog will run right to you every time you call him to come, which is what you want.

Heel

Teaching your dog to heel (walk nicely by your side) makes walking on a lead a fun and enjoyable experience for both of you. It's safer for your dog, because as we learned earlier, small dogs like Yorkies have fragile tracheas that can collapse if too much pressure is put on their little throats.

To teach your dog to heel, connect the lead to your Yorkie's collar or harness and hold the lead in your hand. Bend down and show the dog the treats in your other hand. Move the treat slowly in front of him as if you're leading him by the nose, backing up. Continue walking backward, all the while holding the treat where your dog can see it. As he follows you, praise and reward him.

When your dog follows you nicely, you'll eventually want to turn so that you and your dog are walking side by side, with him on your left side. (Traditionally dogs walk on the left side in shows and other competitions.)

The Expert Knows

Lost Dog

While it's something you never thought would happen to your dog, even the best trained dogs can get lost—a mad dash out the door and suddenly your Yorkie has been gone for hours. What do you do? Don't panic. Here are some things you can do to making finding your dog less difficult:

1 Have your vet implant a microchip into your Yorkie. A microchip is a small rice-sized chip that is injected in between your Yorkie's shoulder blades. Completely harmless, this microchip contains a unique number that, when scanned by a dog warden or rescue centre, refers to a file that contains your contact information.

2 Be sure your Yorkie's collar has an identification tag with all your contact information on it. If someone on the street finds your dog, they can call you and reunite you with your pet.

3 Consider tattooing your Yorkie. Usually placed on the inside of the dog's rear thigh, the number used refers to one of a number of registries.

4 Begin an all-out search. Contact your neighbours, check your Yorkie's favourite play areas, and look for him around your regular walking areas or parks. Put up flyers and signs, and run an advertisement in your local paper or with the local radio station. Visit all your local rescue centres every day, and contact area rescue groups. Notify your vet, too, as well as others in the area.

5 When you find your Yorkie, do not discipline him! If your dog gets out again, he will be afraid to come home. Instead, kneel down and welcome him with open arms. Have a toy or treat to entice the dog. And practice the come command regularly.

6 To prevent the escape from happening in the first place, keep your Yorkie in your sight at all times. If you can't watch him, set up a baby gate or put your dog inside an x-pen with his crate, water, and some toys. You don't want this happening again!

Chapter 7

In the Doghouse

Part of being a well-mannered and obedient dog includes following the rules of the household, set down by you. You are your dog's pack leader, so it's up to you to teach your Yorkie the correct way to behave in the house and with other people. Occasionally, though, problems can occur.

Check with your vet—
some bad behaviour
can be caused by
medical conditions.

Keep in mind that some of the behaviours that we perceive as "problems" are natural to dogs. Yorkies are terriers, and terriers love to dig. Dogs communicate by barking. When their baby teeth fall out, they want to chew to relieve the discomfort. These are all normal dog behaviours. But when temporary behaviours become habits, or when they're done inappropriately, the action needs to be corrected.

How do you do this?

The training we learned in Chapter 6 centred around positive reinforcement. When your Yorkie learned how to sit or stay, he was rewarded with a treat and lots of praise. Eventually, your Yorkie learned to associate good behaviour with praise— which is exactly what you want!

In correction training, you'll use positive reinforcement, but you'll also be correcting your dog when he does something not allowed. You'll need to correct the bad behaviour and reinforce the good behaviour. This can be done in several ways, depending on the particular action that you're trying to correct.

Correction should never include physical punishment. Hitting, shocking or harming your Yorkie in any way is inhumane, and it can create an animal that fears people. Correction, instead, involves getting your Yorkie's attention and stopping the behaviour at that moment.

Tools

One training tool that you'll use— and you have used already—is your voice. The tone of your voice communicates emotion or feeling to your dog. An upbeat higher-pitched tone communicates happiness or excitement. A lower-pitched guttural tone communicates anger or sternness. The dog will respond to these sounds as he would to his mother or pack leader.

So, for example, when you're praising your dog for obeying the *sit* command, you use an upbeat happy tone. Conversely, when you're correcting your dog for barking inappropriately, you use the guttural warning tone. You're not speaking more loudly to the dog, you're using different tones. This means even a soft-spoken person can correct his or her dog.

Another tool you'll need to master is consistency. When you and everyone who comes into contact with your Yorkie requires the same good behaviour from him, he'll not get confused.

Armed with these tools, you're ready to help your Yorkie stay out of the doghouse. Before you begin corrective training, however, check with your vet. Some bad behaviour, such as chronic housesoiling or chewing, can be caused by medical conditions. Other troublesome behaviours can be exacerbated by your Yorkie's diet or lack of exercise. Get a clean bill of health and then begin training.

Some common problem behaviours include housesoiling, barking, jumping up, digging, chewing, and biting/ showing teeth. Let's take a closer look at each one.

Barking (Excessive)

Dogs bark to communicate. From protecting their homes from strangers to trying to get your attention, barking is a natural dog behaviour. Though guarding the home can be a positive reason to bark, your Yorkie's shrill little yap can annoy friends and neighbours—especially if he barks at everything constantly!

Before you begin corrective training, you'll want to determine why your dog is barking. Do you bend

91

In the Doghouse

The Expert Knows

Call in the Professionals

Sometimes your Yorkie's bad habits are just too much for you to handle. You've tried positive reinforcement. You've tried corrective approaches. But your Yorkie still won't stop barking or jumping up on your houseguests. When is it time to seek professional help?

1. If your dog is exhibiting aggressive behaviour, such as biting or showing teeth
2. If his destructive chewing is out of control
3. If the dog cannot be housetrained
4. If he will not obey basic commands, even after puppy class and obedience training
5. If, for any reason, you feel like you can't control your Yorkie, and his safety or the safety of others is at risk

Don't Panic!

A dog with separation anxiety exhibits extreme problem behaviours when he's left alone. After his owner leaves, the dog will dig, chew, or scratch at the door trying to get to his owner. He will howl, cry, and bark, and might even urinate or defecate from distress.

Though dog behaviourists don't know exactly why dogs behave this way, they do know that the dog is not punishing his owner or seeking revenge for leaving. These behaviours are part of a panic response.

Some things seem to trigger separation anxiety. Dogs who are used to being with their owners constantly and are suddenly left alone for the first time may exhibit panicky behaviour. A traumatic event, such as time spent in a rescue centre or kennel, may trigger the anxiety. A change in the family's routine or structure, such as a child leaving for college, could also cause stress in the dog's life.

If you believe you dog is suffering from separation anxiety, here are some ways to correct the behaviour:

- Keep your departures and arrivals low-key. Don't give your Yorkie kisses before you leave and more when you get home. Quietly leave the house and when you return, ignore the dog for a few minutes before acknowledging him.
- Leave your dog an item of clothing that smells like you.
- If your dog chews excessively when you're gone, leave him a chew toy filled with treats.
- More severe cases of separation anxiety require you to systematically train your dog to get used to being alone. Discuss options with your vet and trainer—they may be able to offer more long-term solutions.

over and pick him up every time he barks? Then your Yorkie has trained you! He knows that if he barks, he'll get your attention. Does he bark when someone comes to the door? If so, he is protecting his territory. Does he bark when nobody's home? He might be suffering from separation anxiety (see box, "Don't Panic"). Once you've narrowed down some reasons why your dog barks, you can start correcting his behaviour.

When your dog barks, don't yell at him. To your Yorkie, yelling sounds like barking, and he'll think you're trying to tell him something! Instead, ignore the barking. This may sound difficult, but if your dog realises that he won't get any attention when he barks, he's more likely to stop the behaviour. Reward him for not barking by saying, "Rudy, good dog for being quiet," in your upbeat voice.

Enlist a friend to come to your door and ring the doorbell. Wait until your Yorkie stops barking, saying, "Good quiet," and reinforce the quiet behaviour by praising and treating your dog. Your Yorkie will soon learn that staying quiet will earn him praise.

You'll also want to practice this non-barking behaviour in public. Grab a bag of treats and put your Yorkie on his lead. Walk to the park or somewhere where he barks at people or other dogs. Use the, "Rudy, quiet," command, and if he obeys, lavish him with praise and treats.

Biting and Showing Teeth

There have been many media reports about horrifying dog attacks. While these reports tend to revolve around bigger dogs, even a toy dog needs be trained to never bear his teeth, touch teeth to skin or clothing, or bite. This is one of the most important lessons you can teach your Yorkie.

Mouthing is normal behaviour in puppies. Between 4 to 12 weeks old, your dog learns bite inhibition from his mother and littermates. He learns the amount of mouth pressure that can be used without causing pain or harm by playing with his brothers and sisters, skirmishing, and testing how hard he can bite without causing a squeal. If he is removed from his littermates before learning this inhibition, it is up to the Yorkie's owner to teach him. Start your "No Bite" training as soon as possible to ensure your dog does not develop his mouthing habit into something dangerous. Your Yorkie should know not to bite by the time he is 18 weeks old.

When your puppy nips or bites you, or even just mouths you, say, "Rudy, no. No bite." Stop playing with him and walk away. Do not allow your dog to nip at your heels or chase your feet. This will teach him that biting and nipping result in withdrawal of your attention.

If you find you have a puppy more on the aggressive side, do not play fight, wrestle, or play tug-of-war with

Give your Yorkie appropriate items to chew on.

him. Those types of games encourage aggressive behaviour.

If your Yorkie continues to use his mouth and bite, even after your consistent training, discuss the situation with your veterinary surgeon. He or she may be able to recommend a professional trainer or animal behaviourist who will be able to help you deal with the problem.

Chewing

Chewing, like digging or barking, is something dogs do. When they're between 3 and 6 months old, puppies begin teething, and with that teething comes chewing. They will chew everything and anything. As their baby teeth fall out and their adult teeth erupt, chewing relieves the discomfort. Puppies go through a second chewing phase when they're between 7 and 9 months old as a part of exploring their territory.

Unfortunately, puppies develop a fondness for chewing during these phases. They find out how much fun chewing can be! It relieves tension and anxiety, and it makes their sore gums feel better. For adult dogs, chewing massages their gums, removes plaque, and occupies their time.

Chewing the wrong things, however, can be destructive to your belongings and dangerous to the dog. He could swallow something poisonous, or something small could get lodged in his throat.

Because chewing is just part of being a dog, your Yorkie should have his own things to chew from the

Yorkshire Terriers

FAMILY-FRIENDLY TIP

He's Not a Toy

Sara and her younger sister, Annasophia, love to play with their Yorkie, Ruby. They play hide and seek, toss the dog's ball, and chase each other in the garden while their mother supervises.

But when Ruby started barking and nipping at Annasophia's heels, her mother had to teach her girls that excitable play can cause the pup to react inappropriately. They learned to play calmly around their dog.

Yorkies are little dogs that look like toys to children. They're cute, fun to play with, and a joy to watch. But dogs who have behaviour problems, like barking or nipping, could pose a threat to kids who don't know how to properly handle them.

Here are some tips for combining children with Yorkies—*always* with an adult present, of course:
1. Explain to the child how fragile and volatile the Yorkie is.
2. If the child wants to pet the dog, first have her sit down quietly on the floor and let the dog smell her hand. The child can pet and gently touch the dog if the Yorkie is comfortable.
3. Instruct the child to play calmly and nicely around a Yorkie, especially one with a behaviour problem. Running around and screaming could excite the dog and cause him to jump, bark, and nip.

very beginning. Instead of giving your dog old slippers or waiting until the improper behaviour starts, give him his own size-appropriate chew toys, such as hard rubber balls stuffed with treats, nylon bones, or a rope tug toy. Limit his toys to a few; you don't want your Yorkie to think everything is for his own chewing pleasure! To help him resist temptation, put away items you don't want chewed, especially those that could be harmful to your Yorkie. Those include children's toys with small removable pieces that could be ingested, household cleansers and personal hygiene items, insect and rodent traps, electrical wires, and hobby supplies, just to name a few.

Loneliness and boredom are often the cause of bad behaviour.

Praise your Yorkie often when he chews the right objects. If your dog finds something else to gnaw on, take the object away, and give the dog one of his toys, saying, "Rudy, good toy."

Digging

Yorkies are terriers, and terriers dig. They're bred to hunt vermin, and often those vermin live in holes in the ground. Some dogs dig to create a cool and cozy place to relax, and some dig to get out of a confined area. Instead of trying to teach your Yorkie not to dig, give him a specific place to dig. It will appease those digging tendencies and burn off some excess energy.

Choose a section of your garden and designate it his digging area. Loosen the soil, making sure it is has no pesticides, pieces of glass, or other dangers hidden within. Introduce your Yorkie to the digging area by bringing him over and placing a toy or a treat on the dirt. You could even bury a biscuit or two after he gets used to the area.

When you see your Yorkie digging in the right area, praise him, saying, "Rudy, good dog for digging here." If he digs in other places in the garden and you catch him in the act, move the dog to the right area and praise him when he starts digging there. Bury the other holes and, if you have to, lay some wire mesh over it to discourage further digging.

Housesoiling

You've been taking your Yorkie puppy to his toilet area regularly and letting him relieve himself after every meal, playtime, and nap. Your dog is becoming housetrained. But then, he makes a mistake. What do you do?

The act of relieving himself isn't the mistake; it's going in the wrong place. So if you catch your pup in the

SENIOR DOG TIP

Behaviour Amnesia

Sometimes, older dogs in new homes forget their housetraining habits. The confusion of living in different places and meeting new people causes a temporary doggy amnesia that can be easily remedied. Here are some ways to retrain your veteran dog:

1. Establish a routine. Assume that the dog is not housetrained and set up a routine similar to the one you would establish for a puppy. When he does go outside in his toilet area, praise him with tasty treats and lots of verbal accolades. Use a command phrase, such as "Busy."

2. Supervise. Keep an eye on your older dog at all times and don't give him the opportunity to make a mistake.

3. Confine him or use a crate. As with puppies, older dogs will, by nature, not soil the area where they eat or sleep. Keeping your dog confined in a pen and releasing him on a schedule will get him used to going outside.

4. Mistakes will happen. Do not punish your older dog for housesoiling mistakes. Continue praising him for going in the right place and encourage him with positive reinforcement. If the mistakes continue, however, consult your vet. It could signal a medical problem.

act, say in a corrective tone, "Rudy, no," and immediately take him to his toilet area and let him finish his business out there. Then praise your Yorkie and celebrate that he is going outside.

Clean the soiled area with white vinegar or an over-the-counter pet stain cleaner. Dogs tend to continue soiling in areas that smell like faeces or urine, so removing all traces of the accident will prevent your dog from using that area again.

Don't correct the dog *after* he makes a mistake—he's not able to understand the connection between the correction and the mistake he made hours (even minutes) ago. Also, *never* rub your dog's face in the mess. It's not only an unnecessarily harsh punishment, but your dog will think that you are angry because he defecated, not because he went in the wrong place. Instead, encourage and praise your dog even more when he does go in his correct toilet area. Reinforcing the positive behaviour is the best way to discourage housesoiling.

You'll also want to keep a close eye on your Yorkie. If you know where your dog is, he can't make a mistake. A circling and sniffing dog means he needs to relieve himself, so ask him in an upbeat happy voice, "Rudy, do you need to be busy?" When he runs to the door, take him out and praise him after he goes.

Check out the box "Behaviour Amnesia" for tips on what to do if your older dog regresses in his housetraining.

Yorkshire Terriers

Jumping Up

In Yorkie language, jumping up means, "I'm a happy dog," and "Pay attention to me!" Jumping up means your dog wants to be picked up and made the centre of attention. Thankfully, Yorkies aren't heavy beasts who could knock houseguests over, but this behaviour should still be prohibited.

Just as with excessive barking, it is imperative not to acknowledge your dog when he jumps up. Do not pet him or pick him up, as tempting as it may be! Instead, tell your Yorkie to sit. Only after he obeys should you pet him. Eventually he'll learn that to receive the attention he wants, he'll have to sit, not jump up.

Your Yorkie will also need to learn to sit for other people. Use the lead if you must, and when your guests come to the door and your Yorkie jumps up, say, "Rudy, no jumping," followed by, "Rudy, sit." When the dog sits for a period of time, allow your guests to praise him and give him the attention he wants.

This correction must be done consistently by your family and your friends. Your Yorkie must learn that the only way he will get attention is if he sits first. Praise the dog lavishly every time he does it correctly. Soon, your pup will sit before every greeting.

Oh Behave!

If your Yorkie needs specialised help, you could consider consulting with an animal behaviourist. A behaviourist will take a look at your Yorkie's habits and recommend strategies to correct bad behaviour.

Aggression towards people or other dogs, or severe separation anxiety are the most common reasons that owners seek professional help. In the case of aggression, which is very often provoked by fear, the problem behaviour can escalate very fast. Before you know it you could find yourself in a very difficult and distressing situation.

The best plan is to seek professional help at the first sign of aggressive behaviour. The Association of Pet Behaviour Counsellors is a network of experienced and qualified pet behaviour counsellors who treat problems in dogs. Find out more by logging on to the website: www.apbc. org.uk. In the first instance, you will need a referral from your veterinary surgeon.

Chapter 8

Stepping Out

As a companion and four-legged friend, your Yorkie will probably go everywhere with you. From the grocery store to Grandma's house, you'll want him to show off and strut his stuff. As king of his surroundings, how could he expect anything less? Several competitive venues allow for your Yorkie's pride to prevail.

There are kennel clubs throughout the world, like the Kennel Club (KC) in the UK and the American Kennel Club (AKC) in the US, which offer events for just this purpose. National kennel clubs are national registries of purebred dogs, and they also maintain official records of their sponsored events each year. If your Yorkie is registered with a national club, he can compete in events like dog shows in which canines compete for the best example of the breed; obedience competitions that challenge your Yorkie to a series of exercises that demonstrate his ability to follow your lead; and agility that let dogs demonstrate their athleticism through a series of obstacle courses.

If competition is not for you, there are plenty of other things you can do with your little dog. Yorkies can serve their human friends by working as therapy dogs. Making up games or teaching your dog tricks can also be fun—it's all about finding something both you and your Yorkie enjoy doing together.

Besides competing and game playing, you can take your Yorkie on holiday. Though you'll have to prepare and plan, your dog will love taking in the sights.

Let's take a closer look at how you can step out with your Yorkie.

Agility

What better way for a Yorkie to expend some energy than to participate in agility! This fast-growing canine sport challenges your dog's nimble feet as he runs through a series of timed obstacle courses.

Part of the lure of this fun sport is that dogs of all sizes can compete. The judges adjust the height of the obstacles and vary the time allowance depending on the breed.

There are two agility classes: Agility and Jumping. The Agility Class features contact objects, such as an A-frame and a seesaw. Each obstacle has an area painted on the object, and the dog must place at least one paw in the area to complete the obstacle. The Jumping class has only jumps, tunnels, and weave poles.

Practising for this event can be a challenge, as the obstacles take up considerable space. But clubs across

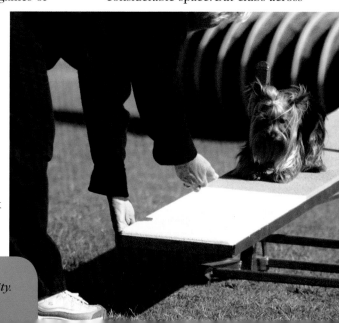

Even your pint-sized Yorkie can excel at agility.

the country conduct training sessions, so if this competition interests you, talk to your local training club for more information or log on to a specialist site, such as www.agilityeye.co.uk.

Good Citizen Scheme

The Good Citizen scheme rewards dogs with good manners. The scheme, which is run by the Kennel Club, has four main awards: Puppy Foundation, Bronze, Silver and Gold. The basic exercises include:

1. Accepting a friendly stranger
2. Sitting politely for petting
3. Appearance and grooming
4. Out for a walk
5. Walking through a crowd
6. Sit and Down on command and Staying in place
7. Coming when called
8. Reacting to another dog
9. Reaction to distraction
10. Supervised separation.

Most training clubs now run Good Citizen award programmes, and if you take on the challenge, you will feel a great sense of achievement as you progress through the levels.

Dog Shows (Conformation)

Most owners think their dogs are perfect. But have you ever considered showing your pet competitively?

Dog shows (also called conformation shows) judge a dog's appearance based on that breed's standard, which we discussed in Chapter 1. To compete in

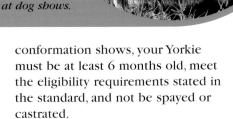

The Yorkie's flowing coat often turns heads at dog shows.

conformation shows, your Yorkie must be at least 6 months old, meet the eligibility requirements stated in the standard, and not be spayed or castrated.

Typically, there are three types of conformation shows: all-breed shows, breed shows, and group shows. All-breed shows, such as Crufts, offer competitions for more than 150 breeds. Breed shows limit the competition to a specific breed. Group shows limit the competition to one of the seven groups, such as the Yorkie's Toy Group.

To get started in conformation show competitions, the first step is to attend a dog show. Usually publicised in local newspapers and hosted by an area all-breed or breed-specific club, these shows will introduce you to the world of showing, give you an opportunity to mingle with other dog owners; and allow you to talk to the club's representatives about how you can join.

Stepping Out

Next, you'll want to attend classes that teach show procedure and etiquette. Your club will have information about classes available in your area. If you don't want to handle your own dog, a professional handler can be hired for a fee. This happens more often in the US; in the UK dogs are generally handled by their owners.

In the United Kingdom, a dog must win three Challenge Certificates (CC) from three different judges, with one of these Certificates being awarded after the age of 1 year. To win a CC, a dog must already have been chosen for Best of Sex.

Although it sounds simple, earning the CC in the United Kingdom is not easy, because not all shows offer these certificates. CCs are allocated by the Kennel Club based on the popularity of the breeds being shown. Additionally, dogs who have already earned a CC can continue to compete for more certificates. It is not uncommon in KC shows for dogs who win frequently at the breed, group, and best-in-show level to never become Champions.

To earn an AKC Champion title, a dog must beat other dogs in multiple age and gender classes to become Winners Dog or Winners Bitch. Based on how many dogs are beaten, points, up to a maximum of five at one time, are earned. Some of the points won must be "majors," in which the dog earns three or more points in a single-breed class. A total of 15 points, with two majors, are necessary to become a Champion of Record.

Obedience

If your Yorkie responded well to obedience training, consider enrolling him in obedience competitions. This sport requires your Yorkie to perform a number of specific exercises that show how well he obeys his handler's commands.

In the UK, obedience competitions are dominated by Border Collies, German Shepherd

Be Safe!

Safety should come first in any activity, especially when engaging in sports like agility, tracking, and flyball. Here are some ways to keep your Yorkie safe:

1. Only participate in activities where your Yorkie feels comfortable. Never force him to do something, like run up a seesaw or through a tunnel.

2. Don't have him jump from high places or compete in trials that might cause him harm. Remember: Your Yorkie is small, and though he is tough, he can easily break bones.

3. Check the field for broken glass, large holes, or other things that could cause injury.

4. Be sure his nails are clipped so they don't catch on anything.

5. Have plenty of water available, especially on hot days.

6. Watch your Yorkie at all times; if it looks like he's in trouble, run to his rescue.

Fresh air and exercise will keep your Yorkie looking and feeling good.

Dogs and a number of the gundog breeds. But there is no reason why your Yorkie should not compete.

Exercises include the following:

- Heelwork on and off lead: As a dog progresses, this becomes increasingly difficult, with numerous turns and changes of direction.
- Retrieve: The dog must retrieve a dumb-bell or an article of the judge's choice.
- Recall: This is a recall to the handler, who may be standing still or moving.
- Stays: The dog must stay in the Sit or Down for a set length of time. In advanced classes, handlers are out of sight.
- Scent discrimination: The dog must pick out a scent cloth with his handler's scent or the judge's scent on it. In advanced classes,

there are also decoy cloths.

- Distance control: The handler must stand at a set distance from the dog and command him to perform a series of moves—Sit, Down, Stand—as the judge dictates. The dog must not move from the area where he is placed.

Other Competitive Events and Games

Other organised events you might find fun include:

- **Canine Freestyle (Dancing With Dogs)**. Canine Freestyle is a human-dog choreographed dance that incorporates obedience commands such as Sit and Stay. Points are awarded to high scores in technical merit and artistic impression.
- **Flyball**. Flyball is a timed relay race that pits teams against each other. This is a great option for small dog owners.

In this game, the first dog must run over hurdles to a box of tennis balls and jump on a lever to send the ball flying. The dog then catches the ball and runs it to his owner. Then the next dog is allowed to go. This fun activity can burn a lot of Yorkie energy! If you are interested, log on to the British Flyball Association website—www.flyball.org.uk.

FAMILY-FRIENDLY TIP

Road Trip!

During summer holidays, 10-year-old Sara and her family travelled to the seaside. Joining them on their journey was their Yorkie, Ruby. It was a long trip, especially for Ruby, who rode in a belted-in carrier. Luckily for the dog Sara was there for entertainment. The two of them watched the miles pass together.

Children and Yorkies can travel together as a team. Responsible young people can be given specific tasks, such as cleaning up after the dog or making sure he is getting enough water. Just because your family is going on holiday doesn't mean the four-legged family member can't come along, too.

- **Games**. Frisbee, fetch, hide and seek, and other games challenge your intelligent Yorkie, encourage positive play, and cement the bond between you and your dog. Plus, they're fun!

Service Opportunities

Well-behaved Yorkies can be trained to become therapy dogs. Pets as Therapy (PAT dogs) is the UK organisation that registers dogs and their handlers to volunteer in hospitals and nursing homes.

Studies have shown that people holding or petting an animal have lower blood pressure and decreased stress. Pets can also pull people out of depression. Your Yorkie brings you joy at home, so why not share that joy with others in need? Watching your Yorkie sit in someone's lap and bring a smile to his or her face is priceless.

Hit the Road

Travelling with your Yorkie can be a fun experience, as long as you're prepared. Whether you're travelling a short distance or across the country, knowing what things to take and how to prepare will make the trip enjoyable for you and your dog.

Short Trips

Short trips to the market delight Yorkies who are used to travelling. The diminutive dog fits snugly in a carrier that doubles as a purse. He can venture into dog-friendly restaurants and shops without anyone knowing. And when he pops his head out, he charms everyone in sight.

If you're taking short jaunts with your Yorkie, you'll need a few things to make it a pleasurable experience for both of you.

Make your dog comfortable in his carrier. Lay down a clean blanket or pillow and toss in his favourite chew toy. Be sure your Yorkie is wearing his collar with ID tag and grab his lead for walks. Stuff a few plastic bags in a side pocket for waste disposal. If you'll be staying away for several hours, consider bringing some of his food, too.

In the car, strap in your Yorkie using a seatbelt harness attached to his carrier, or secure his carrier in the rear of the car. No matter how tempting it is, do not let your Yorkie run free in the car. This is a distraction, putting you and other drivers in danger, and it is hazardous to your dog. If you should stop quickly or get into an accident, your Yorkie could be launched out an open window or be injured.

Long Car Journeys

Longer car journeys will require a little more planning than short trips. You'll need to pack for your Yorkie, prepare any necessary documentation, and talk to your veterinary surgeon.

If you're going by car and your Yorkie has enjoyed the short trips you've made to the shops, he will be used to riding in a car, being strapped in with the seatbelt, seeing all the sights, and smelling all the new smells.

SENIOR DOG TIP

Travelling With Older Dogs

Older Yorkies enjoy car trips just as much as the youngsters, but they do have some special needs you should be prepared for.

1. Before travelling with your older dog, consult your vet. Make sure your dog is fully vaccinated, healthy, and up for the journey.
2. Older dogs move more slowly. Don't be in a rush. Take your time and enjoy the trip!
3. Pack any medications your Yorkie might need, including road sickness remedies and pain relievers.
4. Don't forget his favourite chew toy and comfy bed. Changing an older dog's environment can cause confusion and disorientation, so those comforts of home will calm him.
5. Keep an eye on your older dog. You don't want him to have an accident in the hotel room!
6. Give your Yorkie health checks every day. He should be eating and drinking regularly, but if his appetite or disposition should change, monitor your dog closely.

105

Stepping Out

As you travel, stop every few hours to let your Yorkie relieve himself. Make sure you pick up your Yorkie's messes. Offer your Yorkie water from a portable dish whenever you stop, and if it's mealtime, feed him.

Talk to your vet about any additional vaccinations your Yorkie might need, depending on your destination.

Airplane Journeys

In the UK, it was rare for dogs to travel with their owners on planes, but with the introduction of the PETS passport scheme, air travel for dogs is becoming more widespread.

Airplane journeys require advance preparation. Begin planning at least 30 days beforehand. First, check with the necessary government agency for specifics about what documentation your Yorkie will need at your destination location.

When you make your airplane reservation, notify the airline that you will be bringing a live animal on board. They will ask the dog's size, and whether he will be in cargo hold area or with you in the cabin. Luckily, you're pint-sized companion can travel with you in the cabin—a much safer way than flying him as cargo. He will need to travel in an airline-approved carrier; check with your airline to be sure your carrier is suitable. The airline might also require certain documentation, so be prepared. You don't want your pet to be stranded at the airport!

Overnight Stays

If you will be staying overnight at a friend's house, in a hotel, or on a camp site, prepare accordingly. Some hotels allow pets to stay in the room with you, but they often require an extra security deposit. Call well in advance. Bring your Yorkie's portable kennel or playpen for use in hotel rooms or homes of friends who may not want a dog running loose. You want everyone to be comfortable!

You and your Yorkie can step out in style with proper preparation. Whether it's competing in agility, playing some Frisbee, or going on a car trip, your dog will enjoy the challenge and attention.

Make sure your Yorkie is safe and comfortable in his carrier.

The Expert Knows

Left Behind

• Find out what items from home you can bring. Do they allow you to provide your own food? Can you bring your pup's bed?

• Ask if the kennel will give your dog a flea bath before he leaves to come home. Even though the kennel may be clean, you don't want to risk having to de-flea your house.

No matter how hard it is, there will be times when you won't be able to travel with your Yorkie. Business trips, visiting sick relatives, or a range of other circumstances might require you to leave your dog behind.

In these situations, you'll need to board your dog in a kennel or hire a dog sitter. Here are some tips to make either one a relatively pain-free experience:

Boarding Kennel

• A good kennel can often be recommended by your vet.
• Inspect the facility before you commit. Are the runs large and clean? Do the dogs have full bowls of fresh water? Are the smaller dogs separated from the larger dogs?
• Talk to the kennel manager and staff. Ask what types of vaccinations are required. Do they offer special services, such as individual walks?
• How much experience have they had with Yorkies?

Dog Sitter

• This is often a better alternative than a kennel, as your dog can remain at home in familiar surroundings.
• Dog sitters can often be recommended by your vet.
• Interview several pet sitters before you choose one. Invite them to your home to meet your Yorkie. You'll know right away if your dog likes them!
• During the interview, ask for references, whether he or she belongs to any pet-sitting organisation, how much experience he or she has had with Yorkies, and how long he or she's been a pet sitter.
• Discuss the hours that he or she will be staying at your home. Will he or she feed your Yorkie and leave? Will he or she spend time with your dog and take him for walks? Is he or she willing to spend the night?
• Whether you use a boarding kennel or a pet sitter, be sure to provide plenty of food, treats, and toys for your Yorkie.
• Provide a contact information list: your vets' name, phone number and after-hours number; any medications your Yorkie is taking, the name of a friend or relative nearby; allergies; and anything else you think your kennel or dog sitter will need. Better to be safe than sorry!

Resources

Associations and Organisations

Breed Clubs

American Kennel Club (AKC)

5580 Centerview Drive
Raleigh, NC 27606
Telephone: (919) 233-9767
Fax: (919) 233-3627
E-mail: info@akc.org
www.akc.org

Federation Cynologique Internationale (FCI)

Secretariat General de la FCI
Place Albert 1er,
13 B – 6530 Thuin
Belqique
www.fci.be

The Kennel Club

1 Clarges Street
London W1J 8AB
Telephone: 0870 606 6750
Fax: 0207 518 1058
www.the-kennel-club.org.uk
United Kennel Club (UKC)
100 E. Kilgore Road
Kalamazoo, MI 49002-5584
Telephone: (269) 343-9020
Fax: (269) 343-7037
E-mail: pbickell@ukcdogs.com
www.ukcdogs.com

Pet Sitters
National Association of

Registered Pet Sitters
www.dogsit.com

UK Pet Sitters
Telephone: 01902 41789
www.ukpetsitter.com

Dog Services UK
www.dogservices.co.uk

Rescue Organisations and Animal Welfare
British Veterinary AssociationAnimal Welfare Foundation (BVA AWF)

7 Mansfield Street
London W1G 9NQ
Telephone: 0207 636 6541
Fax: 0207 436 2970
Email: bva-awf@bva.co.uk
www.bva-awf.org.uk/about

Royal Society for the Prevention of Cruelty to Animals (RSPCA)

Telephone: 0870 3335 999
Fax: 0870 7530 284
www.rspca.org.uk

Scottish Society for the Prevention of Cruelty to Animals (SSPCA)

Braehead Mains, 603
Queensferry Road
Edinburgh EH4 6EA
Telephone: 0131 339 0222
Fax: 0131 339 4777
Email: enquiries@

scottishspca.org
www.scottishspca.org/about

Sports
Agility Club UK
www.agilityclub.co.uk

British Flyball Association
PO Box 109, Petersfield
GU32 1XZ
Telephone: 01753 620110
Fax: 01726 861079
Email: bfa@flyball.org.uk
www.flyball.org.uk

Canine Freestyle Federation, Inc.

Secretary: Brandy Clymire
E-Mail: secretary@canine-freestyle.org
www.canine-freestyle.org

International Agility Link (IAL)

Global Administrator: Steve Drinkwater
E-mail: yunde@powerup.au
www.agilityclick.com/~ial

World Canine Freestyle Organisation
P.O. Box 350122,
Brooklyn, NY 11235-2525
Telephone: (718) 332-8336
www.worldcannefreestyle.org

Therapy
Pets As Therapy
3 Grange Farm Cottages,

Wycombe Road, Saunderton, Princes Risborough

Bucks HP27 9NS
Telephone: 0870 977 0003
Fax: 0870 706 2562
www.petsastherapy.org

Training and Behaviour

Association of Pet Dog Trainers (APDT)

PO Box 17
Kempsford GL7 4W7
Telephone: 01285 810811

Association of Pet Behaviour Counsellors

PO Box 46
Worcester WR8 9YS
Telephone: 01386 751151
Fax: 01386 750743
Email: info@apbc.org.uk
www.apbc.org.uk

Veterinary and Health Resources

Association of British Veterinary Acupuncturists (ABVA)

66A Easthorpe, Southwell
Nottinghamshire,
NG25 0HZ
Email: jonnyboyvet@
hotmail.com
www.abva.co.uk

Association of Chartered Physiotherapists Specialising in Animal Therapy (ACPAT)

52 Littleham Road

Exmoouth, Devon EX8 2QJ
Telephone/Fax: 01395
270648
Email: bexsharples@
hotmail.com
www.acpat.org.uk

British Association of Homoeopathic Veterinary Surgeons

Alternative Veterinary Medicine Centre, Chinham House, Stanford in the Vale, Oxfordshire SN7 8NQ

Email: enquiries@bahvs.com
www.bahvs.com

British Association of Veterinary Opthalmologists (BAVO)

Email: hjf@vetspecialists.co.uk
Email: secretary@bravo.org.uk
www.bravo.oprg.uk

British Small Animal Veterinary Association (BSAVA)

Woodrow House, 1 Telford Way, Waterwells Business Park, Quedgley, Gloucester GL2 2AB

Telephone: 01452 726700
Fax: 01452 726701
Email: customerservices@
bsava.com
www.bsava.com

British Veterinary Association (BVA)

7 Mansfield Street
London W1G 9NQ
Telephone: 020 7636 6541

Fax: 020 7436 2970
E-mail: bvahq@bva.co.uk
www.bva.co.uk

British Veterinary Hospitals Association (BHVA)

Station Bungalow,
Main Road, Stockfield,
Northumberland NE43 7HJ
Telephone: 07966 901619
Fax: 07813 915954
Email: office@bvha.org.uk
www.BVHA.org.uk

Royal College of Veterinary Surgeons (RCVS)

Belgravia House, 62-64
Horseferry Road
London SW1P 2AF
Telephone: 0207 222 2001
Fax: 0207 222 2004
Email: admin@rcvs.org.uk
www.rcvs.org.uk

Books

Mini Encyclopedia of Dog Training & Behaviour

Colin Tennant
Interpet Publishing, 2005

What If My Dog...?
Jim Evans
Interpet Publishing, 2006

Index

Yorkshire Terriers

*Note: Boldface numbers
indicate illustrations; t
indicates a table.*

Dedication

For my parents, Drew and Ruth Bedwell, who taught me the value of faith and perseverance.

Acknowledgements

I thank my husband, Ryan, for his continual patience and support; my sister Heather, who showed me how a person can truly make a dog part of her family; David and Candy Taylor, who taught me the importance of humane training techniques; Furkan Niron for sharing his experience and love of Yorkies; Mark Daly, DVM, for medical and training advice; the American Kennel Club; the American Veterinary Medical Assn; scores of reputable breeders, dog trainers and independent pet store owners across the United States for sharing their knowledge of Yorkshire Terriers and proper pet care with me and the public; and my two cats, Star and Benz, who remind me why I love pets.

About the Author

Covering pet and lifestyle topics for more than 10 years, Wendy Bedwell-Wilson has authored hundreds of articles in international consumer and trade magazines, local newspapers and visitor publications, including *Pet Product News, Veterinary Practice News, Cat Fancy, Ponds Magazine* and *Hawaii Magazine*. She also has an editing background, serving as managing editor of several trade, water garden and pet-related magazines. She and her husband, who are both avid dog lovers, live in Hawaii.